SANDRA D. KIRK, PH.D.

THE MYSTERY OF
AVRAHAM'S
LAMB

BEHOLD THE LAMB PUBLICATIONS
Lillian, Alabama

THE MYSTERY OF AVRAHAM'S LAMB
Sandra D. Kirk, Ph.D.
Copyright © 2015

All rights reserved.

No part of this book may be reproduced or transmitted in any form or by any means, electronic, or mechanical, including photocopying, recording, or by any information storage and retrieval system with the written permission of the author. Requests for per-mission should be e-mailed to: beholdministries@outlook.com

Scripture quotations marked *CJB* are from David H. Stern, *Complete Jewish Bible* (Jerusalem, Israel: Jewish New Testament Publications, 1998).

Scripture quotations marked *TLV* are from the *Tree of Life Version of the Holy Scriptures* (Syracuse, New York: Messianic Jewish Family Bible, 2013).

ISBN 9780692518427

Published by BEHOLD THE LAMB PUBLICATIONS

For more information about independent author publishing email: vince@theindieauthors.com

Cover Artist: Christine Leuenberger

Graphic Design: Kirsten Larsen
(www.klarsendesign.com)

Yitz'chak (Isaac) asked, "Father... I see the fire and the wood, but where is the lamb?"

Avraham replied, "God will provide himself the lamb for a burnt offering."

(Genesis [B'rsheet] 22:7-8)

DEDICATION

This book is dedicated to the preservation of Isra'el and the shalom of Yerushalayim (Jerusalem).

CONTENTS

Dedication

Preface: The Story that Changed the World

Glossary of Hebrew to English words

SECTION ONE
Preparing the Seed of Avraham's Lamb

1. **Avraham's Lamb**
   "Father. . .where is the lamb?"

SECTION TWO
The Seed of Avraham's Lamb is Born

2. **Gavri'el's Promise**
   2,000 Years Later on a rooftop in Natzeret (Nazareth)

3. **Midnight** *Sh'khinah*
   The Miraculous Conception

4. **Miryam's Tehillah**
   Two Mothers from Avraham's Seed

5. **Yosef's Dream**
   Eli and Hannah's Grandson

6. **A Baby's Cry**
   The Voice of God Rings Out

7. **Beit-Lechem's Lamb**
   Born to be Slain in Yerushalayim

8. **Bloodbath in Beit-Lechem**
   Miryam's Pierced Heart

9. **"Where Is the Lamb?"**
   Roasting the Paschal Lamb

SECTION THREE
The Seed of Avraham's Lamb Dies

10. **Behold the Lamb**
    Is the Mashiach a King or a Lamb?

11. **ADONAI'S Cup**
    The Second Seder Cup of Judgment

12. **Preparing the Burnt Offering**
    The Meaning of the Holocaust Offering

13. **The Cup of Fire**
    Engulfing the Father's Cup

14. **The Piercing**
    Looking upon the Pierced One

SECTION FOUR
The Seed of Avraham's Lamb Rises and Bears Fruit

15. The Risen Lamb
The First Fruits from the Dead

16. The Ascended Lamb
The Glorious One on the Throne

Epilogue: *ADONAI'S* **Lamb**

Acknowledgements

Contact Information

Other Books by Dr. Sandy Kirk

Endnotes

Preface

THE STORY
THAT CHANGED THE WORLD

This heart-warming story unfolds the Jewish narrative that changed the whole world. Based on true historical events and rooted in Scripture, we will dig between the lines to mine the raw human emotions pulsing beneath the surface. The purpose will be to reach beyond your mind to touch the feelings of your heart.

As you step inside this poignant story, may you feel the love, the passion, the agony, the pain, the fear, and the outbursts of joy kindled in this real-life narrative. Above all, may you experience the presence of ADONAI resting upon you as you read this Jewish novel.

The Story that Changed the World

Before we launch into the story, I must tell you what happened when I researched and wrote these pages. It took me completely by surprise. The *Ruach HaKodesh* (Holy Spirit) came upon me, and I could literally sense the heat of his presence warming my face and moving on my spirit.

Then, when I read it out loud for an audio book, his presence came on me so intensely that I could hardly stand. At the end of some of the chapters, I simply had to put my head down and weep. I know it's because of Adonai's overwhelming love for his Jewish people.

And though written primarily for Jewish readers, today there is a groundswell of love for Isra'el and for God's people among Gentile believers. There is also a mounting hunger to understand our Jewish roots. This is why I have included a Hebrew glossary in the beginning of this book, so that those who don't know Hebrew, can learn the meanings of these words. I will also explain the interpretation in parenthesis until I think you have learned the meaning.

I invite you now to experience the wonder of Adonai's grand love story, planned before the creation of the world. I pray that you too will encounter the *Ruach HaKodesh* flooding over you as together we unravel *the Mystery of Avraham's Lamb*.

GLOSSARY

HEBREW TO ENGLISH WORDS

NAMES

Abba – intimate name for father

ADONAI – LORD

ADONAI Yireh – The LORD will see to it or the LORD will provide (a lamb)

Aharon – Aaron

Avraham – Abraham

Dan'iel – Daniel

Eema – Mama or Mommy

Eliyahu – Elijah

Elisheva – Elizabeth

Gavri'el – Gabriel

Ha'Elyon – God

HaShem – "The Name," the unpronounceable name for God: Y-H-V-H

Hevel – Abel

Glossary

Kefa – Peter

Mamzer – illegitimate child or "bastard"

Mashiach - Messiah

Miryam – Mary

Moshe – Moses

Nakdimon - Nicodemus

Ruach HaKodesh – Holy Spirit

Shi'mon - Simeon

Shlomo – Solomon

Shlomit - Salome

Ya'akov – James or Jacob

Yah – a name of God

Yeshua – Jesus

Yesha'yahu - Isaiah

Yitz'chak - Isaac

Yochanan - John

Yonah - Jonah

Yosef – Joseph

Yosef of Ramatuyim – Joseph of Arimathea

Zavdai - Zebedee

Z'kharyah– Zachariah

Zonah – harlot or whore

Glossary

PLACES

Beit-Lechem – Bethlehem

Galil – Galilee

Gat-Sh'manim – Gethsemane (garden of)

Isra'el – Israel

Mount Horev – Mount Horeb

Mount Moriyah – Mount Moriah

Natzeret – Nazareth

Shomron – Samaria

Yarden – Jordan

Yahweh – the name of God

Yericho - Jericho

Yerushalayim – Jerusalem

Y'huda – Judah or Judea

IMPORTANT WORDS

Akedah – "the binding," referring to the binding of Yitz'chak (Isaac) for sacrifice

B'rit Hadashah – New Testament

B'rakhah – blessing

Cohen – a priest

Glossary

Cohen gadol – high priest

Cohanim – priests (plural)

Emissaries – Apostles

Goyim – Gentiles

Kiddushin – Betrothal

M'chitzah – the wall of separation

Mikveh – a place of washing at the temple

Mishnah – the Oral Law

Seder – Evening meal which begins Passover

Shalom - Peace

Sh'khinah – the manifested presence of God

Talmid – a disciple

Talmidim – disciples

Tanakh – Old Testament

Tehillah – song

Tehillim - Psalms

Torah – First five books of the Old Testament

FESTIVALS AND HOLY DAYS

Hanukkah- Festival of lights

Pesach – Feast of Passover

Rosh HaShanah – Feast of Shofars

Glossary

Shabbat – Sabbath

Shamash – first candle of Hanukkah; the servant or attendant candle

Shavu'ot – Feast of Pentecost

Sukkot – Feast of Tabernacles

Yom Kippur – Feast of Atonement

SECTION ONE

Preparing the Seed

of

Avraham's Lamb

An old man trudges silently up the mountain, his insides heaving with grief. His heart pounds like a thousand horses hooves thundering through his chest.

He pauses to look back over his shoulder at the son he adores. . .

One

AVRAHAM'S LAMB

"Father, . . . where is the Lamb?"

Avraham's throat tightens and his mouth runs dry as he sees his son carrying the wood for the sacrifice over his shoulders. Tears wash the old man's face, soaking into his beard, for he knows he must prepare his son as a burnt offering, just as ADONAI said:

> Avraham . . . take your son, your only son, whom you love, Yitz'chak (Isaac); and go to the land of Moriyah. There you are to offer him as a burnt offering on a mountain that I will point out to you.[1]

But what does this mean? he wonders. *Does* ADONAI *want me to prepare my boy in the way a burnt offering is prepared? Must I slit his throat, splash his*

Avraham's Lamb

blood on the altar, skin him and slice him in pieces, like a lamb for the burnt offering?

He shakes his head, his heart almost convulsing with grief as he further ponders: *Must I arrange the pieces of my son's body on the altar and set him aflame, as required for the burnt offering?*[2]

He lifts his eyes to heaven and quietly prays, not wanting his son to hear: "Oh, ADONAI, surely not! You have promised that you will make a great nation through Yitz'chak (Isaac) and his seed. And now you are asking me to slaughter him like a lamb? This is what the pagans do!"

He sighs heavily, dropping his head, "And yet, not my will, but may ADONAI's will be done."

As Avraham plods on up the mountain, he is lost in thought but determined to obey. He hopes against hope that if he must follow through with this horrific deed, surely God will raise his son from the dead.

Yitz'chak (Isaac) catches up with his father. Breathlessly he asks a stunning question: "My Father, . . . I see the fire and the wood, but where is the lamb for the burnt offering?"

The question stabs his father to the heart. A long, deep, shuddering moan falls from Avraham's lips. He tries to hide the pain on his face as he

Avraham's Lamb

stammers: "My Son, God will provide himself a lamb for the burnt offering."[3]

As they continue to slog along, the autumn sun inflames the sky and blazes mercilessly down upon them. Sweat soaks Avraham's tunic and drips down his neck and back. The wind holds its breath, not a breeze or a gust to cool their heated brows. All of nature seems stunned by this impending sacrifice.

Finally they reach the spot which ADONAI has chosen on Mount Moryah.[4] Avraham silently builds an altar of stones and places the wood upon the altar. Then, with his throat dry and hot tears dripping down his face, he binds the hands and feet of his son and lays him over the wood.[5]

Trusting his father, Yitz'chak (Isaac) surrenders completely to his father's will. But the look in his eyes pierces Avraham to his soul. His eyes seem to ask, "Why? Why are you sacrificing me like a lamb?"

Avraham holds his breath and braces himself. He raises the knife and prepares to plunge it down on the boy.[6] His mind reels and his brain swims with confusion. The thudding of his own blood pulses in his ears. His hand shakes violently as he prepares to slash the blade down across the throat of his son.

But suddenly, he hears something. He freezes. It's a voice from afar, calling, "Avraham. . ."

He looks around. The wind remains silent and still. Birds' songs halt midair. Billowing clouds have gathered, silently churning overhead as though ready to drop a load of tears. But not a sound from nature can be heard. All he can hear is the throbbing of his own heartbeat and the quiet whimpering of his own son, trembling on the altar.

Then he sees a flash of light, brighter than the noon day sun, rushing down from above. Avraham squints his eyes and looks. There, standing in the center of the brilliance, he sees the figure of a man. It is the angel of ADONAI, glowing in the midst of the light and calling, "Avraham? Avraham!"

The old man's heart almost ceases to beat. "Here I am," he gasps.

> Don't lay your hand on the boy! Don't do anything to him! For now I know that you are a man that fears God because you have not withheld your son, your only son, from me.[7]

Emotion bursts in Avraham's heart. He cuts his boy loose, then holds him, weeping wildly. Gut wrenching sobs break from the depths of his being as father and son cling to each other fiercely.

Avraham's Lamb

Then suddenly, he hears behind him an animal sound. Avraham catches his breath and listens. It's the bleating of a sheep—a ram, which is a mature male lamb. He lifts up his eyes and sees the ram's horns entangled in wild myrtle branches and juniper roots. The *Torah* says, "Behold, there was a ram, just caught in the thick bushes by its horns."[8]

A sudden rush of elation erupts from Avraham. He grabs the ram by the horns, slits its throat, skins it, flays it in pieces, and casts it down on the altar. Then he shapes it back in the form of a lamb and ignites the wood.

Even as flames lick the sky and the smoke of the sacrifice curls heavenward, father and son bow together in worship. They weep, they laugh, they shout for joy as together they stretch out their hands to the God who provided a substitute lamb.

Moments pass, and then, without any warning, Avraham senses again that heavenly light. It settles down over him like a soft warm blanket. He lifts his blood shot eyes and beholds the angel of ADONAI, shining in blinding light.

Avraham can hardly breathe past the tautness in his throat. He closes his eyes and listens:

> I have sworn by myself says—ADONAI—
> that because you have done this, that

because you haven't withheld your son, your only son, I will most certainly bless you; and I will most certainly increase your descendants to as many as there are stars in the sky or grains of sand on the seashore. Your descendants will possess the cities of their enemies, and by your descendants all the nations of the earth will be blessed—because you obeyed my order.⁹

Finally Avraham opens his eyes and takes a deep breath. He can hardly take in the wonder of all that God has promised him.

For a moment he pauses to drink in the scene on the mount. The smoke from the burnt offering still spirals heavenward. He breathes in the aroma, knowing that ADONAI himself is smelling this same smoky fragrance.

A fresh tide of faith sweeps over him, inspiring him with revelation. With passion in his voice, he declares that this holy place on the mountain will be named, "ADONAI Yireh." This means, "On the mountain ADONAI will provide,"¹⁰ for indeed, here on this holy ground, God has provided a lamb.

Now Avraham, his face burning with the light of revelation, gazes out from these lofty heights at the land ADONAI has promised is his. He looks to the

Avraham's Lamb

south which will eventually become Y'udah (Judea), with its rugged hills, deep glens, and rocky heights. Then looking north, he views what will someday be clothed with the lush green meadows of the Galil (Galilee) with its rich soil, plentiful vegetation, and sparkling Galilean Sea.

As Avraham looks out from the mount, he knows he stands on holy ground, for there is something divinely significant about this spot which ADONAI has carefully pointed out to him. [11]

Yes, here on Mount Moriyah, where Avraham sacrificed the lamb, King David will offer his burnt offering and fire from heaven will come down. Then David himself will purchase this sacred terrain for the building of a great temple. And here on Mount Moriyah, the magnificent temple of Shlomo (Solomon) will be built as a resting place for the Sh'khinah of God.[12]

The sun is just beginning to sink, staining the horizon with blushes of crimson and gold, as father and son descend the mount. With his heart still vibrating, Avraham thinks how close he had come to slaying his own beloved son. He had almost slashed the blade of a dagger across his throat.

But ADONAI had intervened, for this has only been a test for Avraham. Indeed, God has an infinite plan, for he intends to use the seed of Yitz'chak to change the whole world.

Night slowly falls and Avraham pauses to look up. As he gazes into the dark expanse above him, he stands enthralled. The finger of God has embroidered diamonds of showering stars into the black velvet curtain of the universe, ever reminding him of A<small>DONAI</small>'s eternal promise.

With tears bursting from his eyes, Avraham recalls, *Like the stars that sprinkle the universe, like the grains of sand that cover the seashore, countless children will come from my seed. Through Yitz'chak (Isaac), the son of promise, my descendants will cover this land, and by my descendants all the nations of the earth will be blessed!*

Now, as father and son continue to descend Mount Moriah, arm-in-arm, Avraham leans into Yitz'chak. He feels utterly drained from the ordeal of the last three days. His legs feel weak, his throat aches, and his heart still shakes with emotion. No one can comprehend the magnitude of this sacrifice from a father's heart.

That is. . . no one but A<small>DONAI</small> himself.

SECTION TWO

The Seed

of

Avraham's Lamb is Born

And so the greatest love story of all time begins to unveil. But this is far more than a human love story. It's the narrative of the ineffable love of God for his Hebrew people.

Now let's look ahead, almost 2,000 years later, for finally Avraham's seed has been cultivated and prepared. From the loins of Avraham, through the line of David, ADONAI has carefully nurtured the seed.[13]

Come now to the rooftop of a little stone dwelling in Isra'el, where a young Jewish maiden from Avraham's seed receives a call from God...

Two

GAVRI'EL'S PROMISE

2,000 years later on a rooftop in Natzeret (Nazareth)

She quietly slips from her pallet and tiptoes up the ladder to the terrace on the roof. She leans back against the stone ledge, closing her eyes and drinking deeply of the cool night air. The musky fragrance of saffron, mingled with sweet winter jasmine climbing up the trellis and spilling over the wall, fills her senses.

The early rains of autumn have fallen and winter has spread her chilly blanket over the land. She wraps her shawl, given to her by Yosef at their kiddushin (betrothal), around her shoulders.

She sighs heavily now as she thinks of her beloved, so strong and handsome and desperately tender. Although he is several years older she has admired him as long as she can remember. Not only does his character outshine the other young men of Natzeret, but his great devotion to HaShem has always touched her deeply.

She rises to her feet and leans over the wall of the terrace, looking wistfully out across Natzeret (Nazareth). She sees the winding streets, lined with torches and little shops. The torches flame low, some of them sputtering fitfully, many already burned out. She can almost imagine Yosef's wedding party, bearing torches and crying out, "The bridegroom has come!"

With her heart filled with love, she lifts her eyes to heaven. Sprinkles of starlight, diffusing across the black velvet backdrop of the sky, sparkle like tiny diamonds overhead. She recalls how her father had always taught her—these stars that dazzle the universe forever remind us of the promise A<small>DONAI</small> made to our Patriarch Avraham.

Almost two thousand years ago, from the heights of Mount Moryah, A<small>DONAI</small> had promised, "Because you haven't withheld your son, your only son, I will most certainly bless you, and I will increase your descendants as many as there are stars in the sky or grains of sand on the seashore." He further said, "and by your descendants all the nations of the earth will be blessed."[14]

Gavri'el's Promise

Miryam knows that when at last the Mashiach (Messiah), from the seed of Avraham comes, "all the nations of the earth will be blessed."

Though it was rare for a Jewish girl of her day to learn to read, her father had seen her spiritual hunger as a child, and he had taught her to read the *Tanakh* (Old Testament). From an early age she had memorized many passages from the *Torah*, especially those which spoke of the Mashiach. Often she would pray with all the passion and longing of her heart:

> Oh, ADONAI, how I long for my Mashiach (Messiah)! We have waited so long. When will he come? Our people are severely oppressed. When will he come to overthrow our enemies and set up his glorious kingdom?

Miryam shivers and hugs her shawl more tightly around her. She can hear the sound of crickets chirping in the courtyard and a dove cooing softly to its mate. A lizard scurries over the ledge and disappears in a crack in the wall.

She smiles as she notices several fireflies flashing their tiny lights, darting in and out, winking as though aware of a mysterious secret which is about to unfold.

Then suddenly, without any warning, she hears a rustling sound. A cold chill shudders up her spine. She looks out searchingly across the scene below. It seems as though the whole world stands still. The light breeze ceases. Olive leaves stop quivering. Even the night urchins seem to grow silent.

She listens, her heart pounding in her throat. Then in warm, rich, unearthly tones a voice says, "Miryam."

A flutter of fright sweeps over her. She wheels around to discover the source of the voice. As she turns, a beam of brilliant light strikes her eyes. The vibrant shaft glows brighter and brighter until it becomes like a shimmering bolt. It throbs with life, radiant and supernatural, beyond anything she has ever seen on earth.

She can hardly breathe. Her body trembles. She can feel the quaking starting deep within and quivering through her whole being. Her face drains and beads of cold sweat run down the back of her neck.

The voice speaks again from the shining light: "Shalom, favored one! ADONAI is with you...."[15]

Slowly her eyes adjust to the light until she can faintly make out a hazy presence in the midst of the glory—the figure of a man, enveloped in dazzling,

Gavri'el's Promise

living light. His presence stuns her. Her eyes widen. Her heart hammers. Everything in her wants to turn and flee, but she forces herself to stand, to look unflinchingly into the angel's face.

His eyes flash. Sparks seem to shoot from within them, penetrating Miryam's heart as he speaks. With a solemn look and his arms folded over his chest, he speaks with the authority of one who has come straight from the presence of God. His words take her breath away. She stumbles backwards.

"Don't be afraid, Miryam," he comforts.[16] Then he explains the purpose of his visit. His message is almost too much for her young mind to grasp: "Behold, you will become pregnant and give birth to a son, and you shall call His name Yeshua."[17]

Pregnant with a son? Yeshua? His words shock her senses.

The angel, whose name is Gavri'el, continues, "He will be great. He will be called Son of Ha'Elyon. ADONAI, God, will give him the throne of his forefather David, and he will rule the House of Ya'akov (Jacob) forever—there will be no end to his Kingdom."[18]

Miryam's throat almost closes and she cannot speak. She remembers that beautiful passage in the *Tanakh* (Old Testament), in which ADONAI promises David that his kingdom will never end.[19]

Gavri'el's Promise

She knows that she is a descendant of Avraham and David, and therefore, a child born from her would be of Avraham's seed and David's lineage. But this is almost too much for this simple Jewish girl to grasp.

How could I become pregnant when I'm not even married? she wonders. *I have never known a man. Yosef and I have barely touched hands, and then, only at our kiddushin* (betrothal).

Finally, her head spinning, she manages to stammer, "How can this be, since I am a virgin?"[20]

What the angel says next is a mystery too fathomless to fully comprehend:

> The *Ruach HaKodesh* will come over you,
> the power of *Ha'Elyon* will cover you.
> Therefore the holy child born to you will
> be called the Son of God. [21]

Miryam's heart almost stops. *The Son of God?* she thinks, biting her quivering lip. Her mind reels and strength drains from her body. She can hardly think. *The Son of Ha'Elyon? The Son of God? Does he mean the Mashiach* (Messiah)?

She gasps as it slowly dawns on her. *Me? The mother of the Mashiach? How can this be? I am just a lowly peasant girl from the despised town of Natzeret* (Nazareth). *HaShem would never choose me.*

Gavri'el's Promise

With her mind still swirling, the angel continues, "You have a cousin Elisheva (Elizabeth), who is an old woman; and everyone says she is barren. But she has conceived a son and is six months pregnant!"

Elisheva? she thinks with a sudden gasp. *But she is long past the age of child bearing?* The angel interrupts her thoughts with these striking words of faith: "For with God, nothing is impossible."[22]

When Miryam hears these words, though she doesn't understand, she humbly bows her head and whispers, "I am the servant of ADONAI; may it happen to me as you have said."[23]

Then as quickly as he came, the angel disappears. She rubs her eyes and ponders all the angel has told her. *This must mean that God has chosen me to bear the Mashiach! The Son of God will be conceived in my womb! Oh, ADONAI, this is too much for me to comprehend.*

Excitement fills her as she blurts out loud, "I can hardly wait to tell Yosef! He will be so proud to be the earthly father of the Mashiach!"

But then, slowly and imperceptibly, a dreadful thought forms in the back of her mind: *What if Yosef doesn't understand? What will he think when I become pregnant? Will he think I've been with another man? Will he believe me when I tell him the child is fathered by God?*

Gavri'el's Promise

These thoughts reel through her mind, causing her fears to mount as she considers the worst possible outcome. *Will he reject me? Will he divorce me, which is the only way betrothal can be broken?*[24] She had once heard her father say that, according to oral tradition, "adultery during the betrothal period is a more serious sin than adultery after marriage."

Even worse, will he have me stoned for adultery? She knows the *Torah* says that a woman must be stoned to death if she is found to be pregnant from another man's child. *But I know Yosef would never have me stoned! He loves me too much!*

Finally she cries, "Oh, ADONAI, this is too much for me to understand!" Then, even as she had resolved to the angel, she lifts her hands in utter abandonment. "ADONAI, here I am! I am your servant. May it be to me as you have said!"

And with those words of sweet surrender, she relinquishes all fears. Now, even as the light of the sun swallows up the light of the stars, the afterglow of God's presence swallows up all of her questions. She closes her eyes and slips off to sleep on the rooftop.

Three

MIDNIGHT SH'KHINAH

The Miraculous Conception

"Miryam, Miryam, where are you, Child?"

Rubbing her eyes, she awakens with a start. She bolts down the ladder, "I'm sorry, Eema (Mama). I fell asleep on the terrace last night—praying." Then she halts and catches her breath as she remembers. . .

The memory of last night's encounter with the angel bursts over her conscious mind. Even as she remembers the angel and his astounding message, a rush of glory sweeps over her. Her face shines like the morning sun. *Oh, ADONAI, could it be true?* she thinks with a gasp. A faraway look fills her eyes.

Her mother looks at her quizzically. "Miryam, what's wrong with you? Your face glows like you've seen an angel." *I suppose love affects a girl's sanity*, she thinks, shaking her head.

"Eema, I have," she whispers under her breath, hoping she doesn't hear.

"Ridiculous! Come, Child. We have chores to do."

As soon as her father pronounces the morning b'rakhah (blessing), Miryam scurries through the house, dutifully lighting a fire in the clay oven and preparing the dough for the day's bread. But her thoughts are miles away.

All day Miryam tenderly holds her emotions inside, her heart too full to speak. Then for days afterward, to her mother's consternation, she walks around as though her thoughts are in another world. Every chance she can get, she steals away to pray — weeping, wondering, longing for God to come. Then late one night it happens. . .

After all in the household are asleep, she quietly climbs the ladder up to her trysting place on the roof. For a moment she pauses to look out across her beloved little town of Natzeret, nestled among the fertile fields and rich green slopes of the Galil (Galilee).

Only a few candles still glimmer in the windows. Earlier that evening every family had lit the *Shamash* (servant candle of Hanukkah).[25]

Midnight Sh'khinah

In the light of the stars, she watches the gnarled fig trees spreading wide their leafless branches. Silvery olive leaves shimmer in the starlight, and the feathery leaves of palms whisper in the midnight breeze.

Now, here on this same rooftop where she met the angel, she lifts her face to heaven and prays. The yearning within her rises to the surface and spills out through her words:

> Oh, ADONAI, how I long for my Mashiach (Messiah)! When will he come? How my heart aches for our promised Redeemer. Will he come through me? I believe what the angel said, but I still don't underst. . .

Suddenly, before she could finish her words, she feels a mysterious radiance settling over her. The light increases. It reminds her of the warmth she felt in the presence of the angel, but much more intense, so full of glory and fire. Her heart pounds. Her whole body trembles, for she realizes that this must be the holy *Sh'khinah*, the presence of God.

She catches her breath, inhaling deeply of this heavy, weighty glory. Tears swim in her eyes as light envelopes her. *This must be what the angel meant!* she thinks. Gavri'el had said, "The *Ruach HaKodesh* will come over you, the power of *Ha'Elyon* will cover you."[26]

Miryam feels lost in this inexpressibly holy love. She feels engulfed, utterly suffused by the ineffable presence of Ha'Elyon. It is frightening yet exquisitely wonderful at the same time.

Tears rush down her face. His overshadowing presence is like a divine infusion as he imparts a part of himself into her. It is something holy. Something beautiful. The very seed of God implanted into her womb. Love implodes in her heart.

Moments pass, she doesn't know how long. But finally her heart overflows to Yahweh. She cries, "Can this be happening to me? Have you truly implanted your Beloved Son into my womb? The Mashiach himself enfleshed in a human embryo?"

Slowly now she can feel the intensity of God's glory lifting. She takes a deep breath and opens her eyes, still sensing the afterglow of His lingering presence. Like Moshe's (Moses') shining face when he gazed at the back of God's streaming glory, Miryam's face beams with heavenly light.

Hours pass and she tries to sleep, but it is impossible, so excited, so thrilled is she with the wonder of ADONAI'S glory. She simply lies on the rooftop praying until the first gleam of dawn begins to light the morning sky and spill across the Galilean slopes.

Rising early, before anyone else stirs, she washes her face, changes her clothes, and combs her hair. Her mother finds her, already preparing the morning meal, her face shining with the glory of God.

"Hmmm. . ." breathes Hannah to herself, shaking her head and wondering.

Through the day, Miryam holds her thoughts inside, often touching her stomach and smiling. She almost imagines she can feel the spark of life stirring within her.

Oh if only I could see Cousin Elisheva, she thinks. *If she is already six months with child, as the angel said, then surely she would understand. We could share our miracles together. I don't know if my parents and Yosef will believe me, but I know Elisheva will understand. Oh, I pray that Yosef understands! Surely he will because he loves me and he believes in me so much.*

Later that evening as the lamps are lit and the bread and figs are placed on the low cut table, Miryam announces, "I want to go visit Cousin Elisheva. She is expecting a child, you know!"

"Nonsense, Elisheva is far too old!" growls Eli, her father.

Midnight Sh'khinah

"Abba, nothing is impossible with God," she says quietly, quoting the angel.

"What is wrong with you, Child?" her mother chides, ladling out the soup. "Love does strange things to a girl," she mumbles wistfully.

A few weeks pass and Miryam senses the life of God stirring all the more within her. Already she is beginning to feel some of the early signs of pregnancy. Then one day she says, with a note of fear trembling in her voice, "Eema (Mom), I want to invite Yosef to dinner tonight. There is something I must tell him. . . and you and Abba."

Hannah nods, studying her daughter warily. *Something is wrong, dreadfully wrong,* she thinks. *A mother knows these things.*

That night, after the children are dismissed and the dishes removed from the table, Miryam clears her throat and says shakily, "I have something to tell you."

She swallows hard against the emotion filling her. Yosef leans forward, ready to receive whatever news his beloved bears. Miryam darts a quick glance at Yosef and tries to steady her nerves.

She can hardly breathe past the tightness in her chest as she prepares to break the staggering news to those she loves. Her heart hammers with heavy beats. Her eyes are moist and her face flushed as she says bravely, "I am with child! The Lord has chosen me to carry his Son, the Mashiach (Messiah) of Isra'el!"

Miryam's words strike Yosef squarely in the chest, piercing his heart to the core. His face pales. His stomach drops. His hands clench into fists.

"No-oo!" cries Hannah, bursting into tears and burying her face in her apron. Her father looks at her incredulously. "Impossible," he groans, shaking his head. "Not my innocent little girl. Not you, Miryam." Then, his face darkening, he turns to Yosef and snarls, "How could you violate my daughter?"

Yosef stands, his eyes narrowing coldly. Heat rises in his face. His vision blurs. He barely hears Eli's accusation. "W-who is the father?" he asks numbly, his voice vibrating with wounded love.

Miryam's eyes fill. She rushes to his side and looks deeply into his eyes, tears running unchecked down her cheeks. "Yosef, I would never be unfaithful to you! You are the only man I have ever loved. Please believe me, my Beloved."

Then, through cracking voice, she tries to explain her story. "The angel Gavri'el appeared to me on the rooftop, and told me that I would bear the Mashiach of Isra'el. He said, 'The *Ruach HaKodesh* will come over you. Therefore the holy child born to you will be called the Son of God.' Oh, Yosef, please believe me. It's true. This baby is from the *Ruach HaKodesh!*"

Yosef jerks loose his hands and turns toward the door. "You expect me to believe that! What kind of fool do you take me for?" Charging out the door, he slams it behind him. Out into the night he runs, blinded by tears and rage, stumbling, falling, gasping, screaming like a mad man.

Miryam plunges her face into her hands and sobs. Finally, she looks up at her father and asks softly, "You believe me, don't you, Abba? Eema?" She waits for an answer, but none comes. They simply hold each other, looking down at the floor, as her mother quietly weeps.

"Then I must go see Elisheva!" Miryam says, her jaw set. "Please let me go. I know she will understand..."

"Alright, Child," her father relents. "At least this trip may spare you from public stoning."

"And the humiliation of an unmarried pregnant daughter," murmurs Hannah under her breath.

That night, while tossing on her pallet, she clings desperately to the words of the angel: "Look!

Midnight Sh'khinah

You will become pregnant, and you will give birth to a son, and you are to name him Yeshua. He will be great, he will be called Son of *Ha'Elyon*."[27]

Ha'Elyon — the Son of the Most High. . . Yeshua, the Mashiach . . . she rolls the words over and over in her mind. *I know it's true, no matter what my beloved thinks. No matter what my parents think, he is the Son of God! He is the Seed of Avraham, the promised Mashiach of Isra'el!*

A trace of a smile crosses her face as she thinks, *Soon I will see my dear Cousin Elisheva* (Elizabeth). *I know she will understand this miracle I hold in my womb. . .*

48

Four

MIRYAM'S TEHILLAH

Two Mothers from Avraham's Seed

With heavy heart Miryam bids farewell to her parents and joins a caravan heading south to Y'udah (Judea). "Abba, please tell Yosef good-bye and. . . and that I love him," she sighs. She can feel the tears building behind her eyes but she swallows them down until they become like a rock in her chest.

As the rickety cart pulls out of Natzeret, it passes the town well where the women meet to fill their buckets with water and especially to share the latest gossip. "Shalom, Miryam," someone waves. "Where are you going?"

"I'm going to visit my cousin," she answers, forcing a smile.

"What?" one of the women blurts. Then waiting until she is out of earshot, she whispers, "Miryam is betrothed! She has no business leaving

Miryam's Tehillah

Yosef when she's supposed to be preparing to be wed. Why on earth is she being sent away? Something must be wrong!"

Miryam's stomach sickens, for she senses what they are saying. She knows she is the brunt of cruel gossip, but she straightens her shoulders and looks up. "ADONAI, whatever shame I must endure, thank you for the honor of carrying your Son!"

As the cart rattles down the road, she lets her eyes sweep the Galilean pastures. As far as her eyes can see, lie the olive groves and fruit orchards, now barren of their fruit and leaves.

At night she shivers on the cold hard ground, loneliness engulfing her as she cries herself to sleep. She can hear the wild shriek of jackals and the howling of wolves in the distance. In the mornings, her stomach turns over with nausea.

For almost four grueling days the caravan plods toward the hill country.[28] As they near Shomron (Samaria), the caravan turns eastward, crossing over the frigid waters of the Yarden (Jordan). She can feel the icy cold liquid seeping through the bottom of the cart, freezing her feet.

She knows that Jews cannot contaminate themselves by traveling through Shomron, so they follow the banks of the river until they cross back over into Yericho (Jericho). Then in the distance she

Miryam's Tehillah

sees the hills rising around Yerushalayim. Her blood runs faster now, for she knows her cousin lives in a lovely mountain village just outside the city. She silently prays:

> ADONAI, *this amazing dream will seem more real when I see my elderly, pregnant cousin. Oh, please let her understand when she discovers that I too am with child. Don't let her reject me like all the others.*

The evening sun slopes gently over the hills of Y'udah as the caravan enters the village where her cousin lives. As they near the house, the clatter of hooves on the cobbles draws Elisheva to the window. She squints her eyes to make out the visitor.

"Shalom, my Cousin!" shouts Miryam, seeing her at the window. The moment the sound of Miryam's voice reaches Elisheva, she catches her breath and clutches her stomach. The baby in her womb leaps with a jubilant thud. Never before has she felt such movement from the miracle she carries.

Elisheva rushes to open the door. "Miryam!" she cries, flinging wide her arms to welcome her younger cousin. Instantly, the *Ruach HaKodesh* floods Elisheva and the spirit of prophecy fills her.

Holding Miryam's hands she prophesies, "How blessed are you among women! And how blessed is the child in your womb!" Weeping, she squeezes her tightly and bellows, "But who am I that the mother of my Lord should come to me?"[29]

Kneeling down, the older woman splashes Miryam's feet with warm water, then rubs them with oil. Her husband, Z'kharyah (Zachariah) stands quietly holding the basin of water and a towel. Miryam can feel the hot tears rushing down her cheeks. She sighs and throws back her head, laughing and crying at the same time.

"Oh Elisheva, I hoped you would understand, but how did you know that I too am with child?"

Elisheva rises and with eyes flashing says, "As soon as the sound of your greeting reached my ears, the baby in my womb leaped for joy!"[30] She grabs Miryam's hands and looks deeply into her eyes. "Indeed you are blessed, because you have trusted that the promise ADONAI has made to you will be fulfilled."[31]

Z'kharyah's face beams brightly as he takes in this scene of love and elation between these two women. Miryam sighs and slumps against her older cousin, sobbing like a baby in her mother's arms. Elisheva weeps too, both of them knowing they are caught up together in a master plan which reaches far beyond what either of them can comprehend.

Moments pass and finally Miryam loosens her grip on her cousin. As she straightens, suddenly her heart begins to tremble. Her face shines like a morning sunrise, and with all the passion of her heart, as if the whole world were listening, she bursts into song:

> My soul magnifies ADONAI; and my spirit rejoices in God, my Savior, who has taken notice of his servant girl in her humble position. For— imagine it! — from now on, all generations will call me blessed! . . .[32]

She finishes, and falls back into Elisheva's arms.

Finally, Elisheva motions, "Come, Child, you must be famished from such a long trip." She fills a table with stuffed dates, baked fish, roasted almonds, and a warm loaf of bread. As they eat, Miryam notices that Z'kharyah is strangely silent.

Later that evening, they sit by a fire, sipping mugs of warm, sweet goat's milk. Finally, stealing a glimpse over at Z'kharyah, now peacefully dozing, Miryam whispers timidly, "Elisheva, I don't want to be rude, but why does your husband never speak?"

"Oh, Miryam, it was so amazing!" she smiles. "Let me tell you the whole story. Z'kharyah was offering incense before the great golden altar in the temple in Yerushalayim. Suddenly, an angel— Gavri'el himself, who stands in the presence of God—

appeared to him. He told him that we would have a baby in our old age and we must call him Yochanan (John). ³³ But because my husband questioned the angel, Gavr'el said he wouldn't be able to speak until the baby is born.³⁴

"When he returned home from the temple, I didn't know what to think. His face shone with the glory of God, and though he didn't say a word, he held me and wept."

Elisheva blushes and looks down, then continues. "He began smothering me with kisses like a young man with a new bride!" Her face reddens even brighter, and Z'kharyah, who by now is awake and listening, blushes too, breaking into a boyish grin.

"He was so loving and persistent and my heart soon melted like a young bride. Then, to my utter shock, I soon became pregnant!"

"After that, I watched Z'kharyah immersing himself in scrolls from the *Tanakh*, pouring over Scriptures late into the night. Often I would see him wiping away tears as he grappled with verses which he only vaguely understood."

Bubbling over with excitement, she suddenly exclaims, "But not until this evening—not until the babe leapt in my womb and you and I both

Miryam's Tehillah

prophesied—did he fully put the pieces of the puzzle together."

Suddenly, a deep shuddering sigh heaves from Z'kharyah as an onrush of revelation sweeps over him. He looks as though he has swallowed a great secret, a divine mystery which God is unveiling to him in that moment.

He picks up a tablet and with deep emotion he writes: "IT IS TIME!" The two women look at him curiously and he writes three numbers: "14 - 14 - 14."

Elisheva knits her brow and ponders these numbers. Then her husband writes, "Avraham - David - Dani'el... *Mashiach!*"

Suddenly, the older woman takes in a quick gasp of air. "Ah, yes, it has been fourteen generations from Avraham to David, fourteen generations from David to Dani'el in captivity, and now fourteen generations from the captivity until the present time! It is time for the Mashiach to be born!"[35]

Z'kharyah's face gleams. He opens the scroll of Mal'akhi (Malachi), and Elisheva reads, "Behold, I am sending my messenger to clear the way before Me."[36] Though he does not speak, his face glows as bright as Miryam's with the sacred inner fire.

Then he quickly opens the scroll of Yesha'Yahu (Isaiah) and points to a passage. Elisheva reads, her voice trembling, "The prophet says, 'A voice cries out in the wilderness, Prepare the way of ADONAI, make straight in the desert a highway for our God.'³⁷

"Miryam, do you see? The angel told my husband that our son would prepare the way for the Mashiach and these verses in the *Tanakh* confirm it."

Z'kharyah shifts in his chair. Miryam and Elisheva glance at him and see tears running down his venerable face, disappearing in his beard. He rises slowly and points to another passage in Yesha'Yahu (Isaiah). Elisheva reads the text for him:

> For to us a child is born, a son will be given to us, and the government will be upon his shoulder. His Name will be called Wonderful Counselor, Mighty God, my Father of Eternity, Prince of Peace.³⁸

Z'kharyah smiles broadly. With eyes sparkling, he lifts up his tablet and points again to the words, "IT IS TIME!"

Elisheva throws her arms around Miryam and cries, "Oh, my little Miryam, do you know what this means? The *Tanakh* has spoken. The time has truly come. It is time for the Mashiach to be born upon this earth, and ADONAI has chosen you to bring him forth!"

Miryam's Tehillah

Elisheva looks deeply and solemnly into Miryam's eyes. "My Child, ADONAI has given you a high and holy calling. Never forget, no matter what you must suffer for him, you are bearing to this earth our Jewish Mashiach—the seed of Avraham—the very Son of God!"

The months pass quickly, and soon the time draws near for Elisheva's travail. Miryam is over three months pregnant now, and she knows it is time to return to Natzeret. She arranges to join a caravan, heading north, and then tearfully bids them farewell.

On the first day of her long journey home, her hopes soar high, but as the days wear on, her courage sags. Worry tugs at her heart.

Why haven't I heard anything at all from Yosef? What will he think when he sees me? How will he feel about my bulging stomach? Will he have compassion or will he be repulsed? Will he want to divorce me, since betrothal can only be broken through a legal writing of divorcement? What if he wants me stoned for adultery?

As the donkey trudges along the dusty road toward Natzeret, she wonders, *What about my parents? Will they be too ashamed to take me back in? If they cast me out, I will be left homeless and alone. What of the baby?*

Miryam's Tehillah

Day after day, she wrestles with these tormenting thoughts, while listening to the endless clicking of donkey hooves plodding along the road.

Finally, they draw near the outskirts of Natzeret. As they pass the well, the women scowl. "Look, it's Miryam. . . See how her pregnancy shows!" "Poor Hannah and Eli! Such disgrace she has brought to them and to Yosef." "Why, that girl should be ashamed to show her face in this town!"

Suddenly, Miryam feels a sharp blow to her temple. Blood streams down her cheeks. A boy has hurled a stone at her, yelling, "Zonah (Harlot)!" Then he scampers away giggling.

When the caravan leader hears this, he realizes that he has an unwed pregnant girl among them. He stops the cart and snarls, "Get out!" Cursing under his breath, he mutters angrily, "She can walk the rest of the way! Serves her right!"

Lugging her bag over her shoulder, she slips off the cart and treads wearily up the pathway to her parent's house. When she nears the little dwelling, the children playing outside squeal, "Miryam's home!" They run to her and smother her with kisses.

Word reaches her parents and they rush to meet her. "Miryam, my Child! Oh, what has happened to you?" her mother shrieks when she sees the blood on her face.

Running eagerly toward her daughter she throws her arms open wide. Then she looks down at her protruding belly and halts.

"Oh, no! Then it *is* true!" she whimpers, clenching her hands into knots. Her face darkens as she cries bitterly, "Such shame you have brought on us, Child!"

"Have you seen Yosef?" she asks anxiously. At this her parents stiffen and look down. The long silence that follows causes Miryam's heart to sink.

Finally, her father clears his throat and says, "His father says he is preparing to divorce you privately."

"Oh, no!" Miryam wails. "How can that be? He loves me and I love him!"

"You should be grateful that he doesn't want to publicly divorce you for adultery, which would require stoning!" blurts Eli. Hannah nods.

"Grateful?" She looks at her parents, hot tears scalding her cheeks. "Then you, my own parents, still don't believe!" She squares her shoulders and clutches her stomach. With eyes blazing she proclaims, "This child *is* from the *Ruach HaKodesh!*"

Miryam's Tehillah

Rushing to the ladder leading up to the roof, she starts to climb, then stops and looks back over her shoulder. "And by the way, our cousin Elisheva *is* with child. She is soon to give birth to a boy. She says his name will be Yochanan (John)."

Then lifting her tear stained face, she announces, "*ADONAI* showed Elisheva and her husband the truth through the Scriptures. Their son is to be the forerunner of the Mashiach, and my son is none other than the Mashiach himself! The very Son of God!"

Five

YOSEF'S DREAM

Eli and Hannah's Grandson

"No!" screams Yosef, sitting up on his pallet, his clothes drenched with sweat, his thin blanket twisted around him.

Every time he closes his eyes he sees Miryam with another man. Or worse, he sees people hurling stones down upon her, maiming her beautiful flesh and shouting "Adulterer!" "Zonah (Harlot)!" Since the night she made the announcement, "I am with child," he has barely slept.

He flings off the covers and jumps up, restlessly pacing the floor. *Oh, Miryam, I can't get you out of my mind! Surely, love drives a man mad!* His heart heaves with torment. His fevered brain reels in confusion.

My precious Miryam, how could you wound our love so deeply? He has loved her almost beyond reason, but now, like a storm-tossed boat dashed against jutting rocks and splintering into a million pieces, all of his dreams of marriage and family have been shattered and strewn on the lonely shores of his life.

How could she betray me like this? I loved her so. I would have given my life for her. She said she loved me too, but now I see it was all a sham. She only wanted a name for her baby.

He throws himself back down on his pallet, beating his fists into his pillow. Waves of darkness sweep over him. Over eight months have passed since Yosef has seen her.

He knows she has returned from her cousin's home in the hill country, but he hasn't gone near. By now, she would be heavy with child. The sight would be revolting, heart-breaking to this grief-torn lover.

He has put the divorce off as long as possible, finally applying for it a few days ago. He will divorce her privately to avoid public exposure.[39]

Though he knows Miryam has surely endured her own humiliation, no one can know his own private hell.

I've become the laughing stock of Natzeret! The brunt of endless jokes. "There goes the carpenter who is

Yosef's Dream

betrothed to a zonah (harlot)," they whisper, but I always know what they're saying. Some even accuse me of being the father. *"Yosef just couldn't wait! Now he's too proud to admit it!"*

But worse than the gossip is the emptiness he feels. His heart aches with the pain of his loss. And though he tries to turn to the Lord in prayer, ADONAI seems strangely distant to him these days.

Tossing fitfully, he finally drops off into an exhausted sleep. Suddenly, in a dream, a supernatural presence invades his sleep. He sees a light glowing brighter and brighter, and within the light stands a man. The man is an angel, shining in pulsing, living light.

Yosef hears him speak in what seems like an audible voice. He says, "Yosef, son of David, do not be afraid to take Miryam home with you as your wife; for what has been conceived in her is from the *Ruach HaKodesh*."[40]

A profound peace floods his soul as the angel continues: "She will give birth to a son, and you are to name him Yeshua, [which means 'ADONAI saves,'] because He will save His people from their sins."[41]

Yosef awakes with a start. The presence of God rests heavily upon him. Remembering his dream, he thinks, *"The angel said that what has been*

Yosef's Dream

conceived in her is from the Ruach HaKodesh!" He throws back his cover and cries, "Dear Lord, this baby *is* from you! I have been so wrong!"

He leaps from his pallet, splashes himself with water, throws on his tunic, and races out into the street toward Miryam's house.

The crimson glow of dawn has just begun to peek over the horizon as he runs breathlessly up the winding road.

A few drowsy vendors are already beginning to set up their wares along the street. Several torches still burn restlessly, most standing cold and flameless. But the flame in Yosef's heart burns strong, fueled by the oil of love and the grief of remorse.

"Oh, Miryam, I didn't believe you! My precious little Miryam, my beloved!" he moans, tears stinging his blood-shot eyes as he stumbles up the path.

What will I say when I see her? Oh, I'm so ashamed! I promised at our betrothal to protect her and faithfully stand with her through all trials, but I ran out on her.

I doubted her. How can she ever forgive me? How can she ever respect me as a man when I've been so easily deceived, thinking only of my feelings, not hers?

Yosef's Dream

When he finally reaches her home, he almost wants to break through the door, but then checks himself. *Where are your manners, Yosef?* he scolds.

He respectfully touches the mezuzah on the door post and knocks. Then, forgetting himself, he pounds on the door, frantically calling her name.

Hannah opens the door cautiously, and he bursts into the little room, breathless and glowing. His eyes search the house for his beloved.

There she stands, kneading dough for the morning meal, ringlets of dark hair hanging over her face. She looks up in shock. Her face looks drawn and pale, frightened by this explosive intrusion.

What does he want? Has his pain driven him mad? Taking a step back, she flings back her hair and wipes her hands on her apron.

Yosef starts toward her, then freezes, paralyzed by love. He searches her dark liquid eyes, looking for a flicker of love.

She looks away quickly, her face blushing, hoping to hide her pain. Her heart feels cold and numb, almost unable to feel anymore.

"Oh, my Beloved. . ." he finally stammers. He lunges forward and falls at her feet. "I am so sorry! I doubted your purity. I didn't believe you, and I was so wrong!"

Miryam looks at him with hurt. She has cried many tears over this man she has always loved — who deserted her when she needed him most. Now her heart feels cautious, almost cold.

But gradually, as he spills out his love and remorse, her icy heart begins to warm . . . and finally to melt.

Still kneeling, he looks up into her eyes, speaking with firm resolve, "Miryam, this child you carry is from A*DONAI*! The Lord has chosen you to be the mother of the Mashiach!"

He pauses and swallows hard, softening his voice. "Miryam, he has given me the honor — that is, if you will have me — of being his earthly father. I want you to be my wife, my Beloved, if you can forgive me."

Then he covers his face in his hands and sobs, "Please, please forgive me. . . "

She hesitates, then whispers, "Yosef, you are the only man I have ever loved. I do forgive you. I prayed the Lord would show you, but I've missed you so desperately!"

Yosef's Dream

His eyes light up and he stands to his feet. Everything in him wants to enfold her in his arms, but he knows he must not break protocol. He must honor the purity of betrothal, and so without even touching her, he loves her with his eyes.

"I need you, Yosef," she whispers. "I cannot bear to live without you."

The rest of the household stands back shocked and silent as both Miryam and Yosef bow their heads and weep. They weep for all the pain they have suffered. They weep for joy, the sheer joy of reunion. They weep for love.

It is as though all the sorrow of the last eight months spills out of their hearts, washing away their pain through the power of forgiveness and the light of their rekindled love.

Finally, Yosef, looks up, his face beaming. "I almost forgot, Miryam. We must give Him the name of *Yeshua*."[42]

"Yosef, how did you know? That's what the angel told me to name him!"

"He told me, too, my Beloved—in a dream which was from ADONAI."

Eli suddenly breaks in dryly, "How do you know it was a dream from ADONAI? Dreams can be

Yosef's Dream

from anything." Miryam's father had always been a practical man, a student of the Scriptures and not easily impressed with spiritual experiences. "Only fools follow dreams," he smirks.

"Sir, respectfully I must disagree. This was not just any dream. I went to sleep in torment and pain. I awoke from my dream with a peace like I'd never known. It was the presence of God, resting heavily upon me."

As he spoke, everyone listening could feel the presence of the *Ruach HaKodesh* filling the room.

"Even so, I don't believe it!" Eli retorted, shaking his head. Everything in him wanted to believe that what Yosef said was true. Most of all he longed to believe that his daughter was innocent of adultery. This was his little girl. His firstborn.

But all this talk of angels and glory and dreams seemed like nonsense. He once heard of a woman who claimed to be pregnant with the Mashiach and it was sheer fantasy. A silly woman's folly. She wasn't even pregnant and she disgraced her whole family with her fanciful delusions.[43]

Turning his eyes back to Miryam, Yosef says, "Tomorrow we will go to the rabbi and be privately wed. Then we must travel together to Beit-Lechem (Bethlehem) in Y'huda."

Yosef's Dream

"Beit-Lechem!" shrieks Hannah. "No, you can't. The time of your travail will be upon you soon. You don't dare be so far from home at such a time."

"We must go, Miryam. Caesar Augustus has issued a decree for a census and we must go before the baby comes. We must register in the town of my lineage, the City of David—Beit-Lechem."

Eli gives a sudden gasp and grows very quiet. He strokes his beard as though deep in thought. "Beit-Lechem...." he mutters with a faraway look on his face. *"Beit-Lechem?"*

A long tremulous sigh falls from his lips. He looks at his daughter, stunned, as though suddenly slapped in the face. It's as though he sees her, really sees her, for the first time in months.

A hush falls on the room as everyone turns toward him, waiting for him to speak.

His eyes shine, moistened with tears, and he tries to speak but words stick in his throat.

Finally, he clears his throat and speaks, softly at first, "The prophet Mikhah (Micah) writes, 'But you, Beit-Lechem near Efrat, so small among the clans of Y'hudah, out of you will come forth to me...'"

Eli's voice cracks and the tears begin to fall. "'Out of you will come for me the future ruler of

Yosef's Dream

Isra'el, whose origins are far in the past, back in ancient times.'"⁴⁴

Then with glory shining on his face, he adds his own thoughts, "whose origins are as far back as Avraham himself!"

Walking slowly and painfully across the room, he takes Miryam's hands and, through chokes and sobs, he quotes Yesha'Yahu (Isaiah): "Behold, the virgin will conceive. When she is giving birth to a son...."⁴⁵

"My daughter," he cries, his face scarlet with contrition, "I believe! This child *is* the coming Redeemer. He *is* the eternal Son of God, the ruler over Isra'el—our long awaited Mashiach!"

He buries his face in her shoulder, deep sobs racking his whole body. "Miryam, I believe! I believe! Forgive me for ever doubting you—my pure and innocent child. Adonai's chosen one."

Finally, straightening himself, he brushes away tears and clears his throat. Placing his hands on Yosef's shoulders, he says, "Please forgive me, my Son, for accusing you and doubting your honor. This child is indeed the Mashiach, conceived by the *Ruach HaKodesh*, and Adonai has chosen you to be his earthly father."

Yosef's Dream

Hannah looks on half dazed. *How can this possibly be true?* she wonders. *I'm not moved by Scripture as my husband is. . . No! I refuse to believe it! I've suffered far too much disgrace to cave in to such prophetic sand castles!*

Then suddenly, the boisterous voice of Hannah's sister barging through the door crashes through the emotion-charged atmosphere of the little hut. "Have you heard the news?" she squawks.

Miryam and Yosef look up surprised. Eli, obviously agitated, groans to his sister-in-law, "Not now, D'vorah!"

"No, listen," she cries, half crying, half laughing. "Our dear old relative Elisheva has had a baby! Can you imagine—a baby at her age! A little boy. . . ."

Hannah stiffens. Her eyes widen and her face turns white.

"Can you believe it?" she chortles. "He was born a few months ago, we just hadn't heard the news up here in Natzeret. They say his name is Yochanan (John)!"

A tear starts down Miryam's cheek. She leans closer to Yosef and quietly weeps.

Yosef's Dream

"What? Yochanan!" screeches Hannah, shock sweeping over her. She weaves unsteadily as though ready to faint, and Yosef reaches out to help her. Recovering herself, she catches her breath. "Th-that means...."

A scream tears from her throat. She rushes to Miryam's side, weeping wildly. "Oh, my child, my poor child," she cries, grabbing Miryam's hand. "I am so sorry I've been so blind! It's this wretched pride of mine! I have been too caught up with my own shame to believe you."

"Now I know it's true. Everything you tried to tell me... the angel, your baby, Elisheva's child... It's all true! Oh, my precious daughter, you have truly honored this house by being the chosen one!"

Then Hannah pauses and closes her eyes as though struck again by a sudden epiphany. Her face glistens as revelation sweeps over her like waves of a sea, lapping over the shore of her heart. Tears run unchecked down her wrinkled face.

A thick silence fills the room again, as everyone waits to hear what she will say. Finally she opens her eyes, her face beaming. She tilts her chin high and struts over to her husband.

Yosef's Dream

Placing her hands tenderly on his time-weathered face, she crows, "My dear husband, do you know what this means?"

She hesitates, waiting for her words to sink in. He looks at her curiously. Then triumphantly she announces, "Our first grandchild will be the Son of God! The *Mashiach of Isra'el!*"

Six

A BABY'S CRY
The Voice of God Rings Out

The day dawns clear and crisp and filled with expectancy. Bidding farewell to their parents, Miryam and Yosef promise to come home soon, unaware that it will be years before they can safely return.

Traveling south, then turning east and crossing the chilly waters of the Yarden (Jordan), they turn back south along the banks of the river. At night they huddle together by a fire, drawing strength from their God and one another.

As Miryam gazes into the flames, a fresh rush of gratitude overwhelms her. Her eyes fill with tears as she thinks, *Abba believes! Eema believes! Most of all, my Yosef believes and we are together at last!*

Each morning, as Yosef lifts Miryam up to the donkey, her discomfort intensifies. As the donkey

A Baby's Cry

lumbers down the road, she can feel his heaving sides. With every jarring step her insides jolt. She holds her stomach, as though to protect her baby, but her thighs ache and pain throbs through her body. *I can't tell Yosef how I feel,* she thinks. *He already has enough on his mind. I don't want to worry him.*

Though filled with joy, the trip is slower and harder than usual, for Miryam has to stop and stretch and walk. Finally they cross into Yericho (Jericho) and enter the hill country of Y'udah.[46]

Now suddenly, the roads throng with people, swarming in from the hills and adjoining roads, heading toward Beit-Lechem to register in the census.

I didn't expect such a crowd, Yosef thinks. *I have enough shekels to pay for a room in the inn, but what if there's no room? And what if her travail starts? How will I ever find a midwife to deliver the baby in this teeming mass of humanity? Who then will deliver the child?*

Yosef's face reddens and his palms, holding the donkey's reins, begin to sweat. *Why didn't I think of these things,* he worries, blushing with shame. *Please, Adonai, help me,* he silently screams. *Oh, how I wish Hannah were here!*

"Yosef, what's wrong?" Miryam calls, sensing his dread.

A Baby's Cry

"All is well, my Beloved," he assures, forcing a smile. "We will be there soon."

They plod along in silence, Yosef's head swimming, his mind trying to think what to do. *If there's no room in the inn, I can't let her sleep out in the open fields. If the baby comes, I can't let her be exposed to the gawking eyes of strangers!*

Suddenly, Miryam screams a piteous cry that stabs his heart, "Yosef!" He rushes to her side, where she motions for him to lift her off the donkey. His face blanches as he sees the blanket where she has been sitting, soaked with the waters of childbirth.

He holds her until the contraction passes, then he places her back on the donkey. She has been having small contractions for the last few hours, but hasn't said anything. "We must hurry, Yosef," she cries. "The pains are getting worse."

Yosef's heart races as he steps up the pace, elbowing his way through the crowd, and tugging hard on the reins of the exhausted donkey. "My wife is in travail! She is about to give birth," he cries, his face flushing crimson red, but the people grunt and shove and pay no attention.

The sun is just beginning to drop toward the western hills as Yosef shouts, "Look, there it is!" They strain their eyes to see in the distance the small

A Baby's Cry

town of Beit-Lechem, nestled on a plateau which spreads in an extended strip over the crest of Y'udah.

As they draw closer, they can see gnarled grape vines covering the undulating terraces. Flocks of sheep graze lazily on the hillside.

Finally, reaching the city entrance, another contraction comes. But the press of teeming, sweating humanity leaves no room for Yosef to lift her to a place of rest.

Enduring the pain on the back of a donkey, Miryam pants hard, groaning and gripping Yosef's hand till her knuckles turn white. When the pain passes, Yosef looks above the crowd and spies the inn. He tethers the donkey to a post, promising to return as quickly as possible.

Fear grips him as he begs for a room. "Sorry, all full! Now move along, Son."

"Please, Sir, my wife is in the throes of childbirth! We need a midwife and a private room," he cries desperately. "Too bad, you'll have to sleep in the open field," the innkeeper responds heartlessly.

"What's that?" breaks in the innkeeper's wife, catching the last bit of Yosef's plea. She looks at him with compassion. His face is strained, streaked with tears and dirt, and his eyes plead for mercy.

A Baby's Cry

"Did you say your wife is in childbirth? Avner, come now, we can surely find some place for them to have their baby in peace."

The innkeeper rubs his brow and thinks. "Hmm... There is a little cave on the hill which we use for a stable. I put some fresh straw in there this morning. If you'll build a fire, your wife will be warm and secluded from the stare of intrusive eyes. You're welcome to bed down there if you can endure the stench."

"Oh thank you, Sir, but we also need a midwife. Can you send one to us? I can pay her whatever she wants."

"Mercy me, Son," the innkeeper's wife breaks in. "We would never be able to find a midwife at a time like this. But don't worry, the Lord will be with you. Here's plenty of rags and soap and a few blankets. You'll need them when you deliver the baby."

Yosef's face drains and his mouth runs dry. *Me? Deliver the baby? But I am a man, and I know nothing of these things! And surely, it is not proper for a man to look upon childbirth! Dear God, this is too much for a mere man!*

A Baby's Cry

"Oh, please M'am, couldn't you help us? I know nothing of these things," Yosef says desperately.

"Sorry, Son, our inn is bursting at the seams and the guests are clamoring for my help. But I'll bring some hot water as soon as I can."

"Here, young man, take this torch to light the way as darkness is quickly falling. You can use it to help start a fire," says the innkeeper, his voice now soft with compassion.

Wiping his brow, Yosef straightens his shoulders and returns to Miryam, trying to look confident. "The inn is full, but I found a place. A warm little cave down the hill. It will give us the privacy we need."

"But Yosef, who will help me? I thought we would have a midwife! Oh, I wish my mother were here!"

"Don't worry, my Dove. I will be with you," he says bravely. "And most of all, ADONAI is with us!" Another contraction hits her and she shudders in pain, clenching Yosef's strong hand until it passes.

Darkness has fallen by the time they find their way down the winding path to their humble abode on the hillside. The clear sky overhead glistens with starlight, but one dazzling star burns brighter,

A Baby's Cry

illuminating the path with streaming, almost supernatural light. It even seems to hover over the cave.

Yosef notices and, pointing toward the star, says cheerily, "See, Miryam, HaShem is showing us we are not alone. He is lighting our path all the way." They both look up and it almost seems as though a sudden flash of scintillating starlight sparkles down on the little stable.

They enter the cave, where Yosef drives the stake of the torch into the ground, illuminating the darkness. He sees a pile of hay, lying inside by the entrance. He clears out a spot for Miryam and covers it with fresh hay and blankets. Then he lowers her to the makeshift bed.

Immediately, another pain strikes and she writhes in agony as though her very bones are opening to give way to this wonderful miracle.

When the pain subsides, he holds up her head and gives her a few sips of water. Then he hurries about, gathering twigs and branches for a fire. Soon hot flames crackle, warming the cave and transforming it into their own little palace.

For a moment, Yosef stares into the mesmerizing flames and prays:

A Baby's Cry

A̲d̲o̲n̲a̲i̲, I'm beside myself with excitement... and fear. Please help me. I am only a man. I don't know about these things. Please send your angels to help me in this mighty task, for this is your Son! Surely you will be with me... and with Miryam and the baby. Please help us in this miracle of birthing the Mashiach to the earth.

He gazes around the humble little cave. The air reeks with the pungent scent of urine and the stench of oxen dung. The flames cast animal shadows against the stone walls of the cave. He cleans out a manger, which is an animal feeding trough, filling it with fresh hay.

Then he sits back down in front of the fire and prays, "Oh A̲d̲o̲n̲a̲i̲, your Son should not be born in such squalor. The Mashiach is fit for a temple or the chambers of a king, but certainly not an animal stable."

He grits his teeth and to himself he thinks, *I feel so ashamed. I was supposed to provide for her and protect her, and all I can give her is a filthy animal stable for his birth, a feeding trough for his bed.*

Just then the innkeeper's wife calls out from the mouth of the cave, startling him from his thoughts and prayers. "Here, Son, I've brought you plenty of

A Baby's Cry

hot water and some nice warm lentil soup. When the child is born, your wife will need her strength."

"Thank you so much, but couldn't you please stay? My wife is very close to giving birth," he pleads.

"Sorry, Son, but don't worry. You'll do fine. The Lord will help you." She turns and hurries back towards the inn.

Yosef's head spins. *Oh, God, help me, please!* Returning to Miryam, he smiles confidently and holds her head up for a sip of cool water. He strokes her black silky hair, now matted and wet with sweat. He mops her brow and lays her back on the hay.

"Yosef, I'm frightened," she moans.

"Don't be afraid. God is with us. This is his Son, and he will protect you and his little one," he says, still hoping the tremor in his voice does not betray the terrror that grips his heart.

Yosef stirs the fire and puts on fresh wood to keep the water hot. Though his stomach twists into knots, he remains outwardly calm, a source of strength for Miryam. Knowing her time is near, he washes his hands with soap and hot water and returns to her side.

A Baby's Cry

He finds her thrashing about in the hay, in the throes of pain. Finally, she pants breathlessly, "Yosef, the pains are getting closer now. The time is almost upon us." She tries to say more but the pain is too deep for words. She grips Yosef's hand fiercely.

Another long contraction. Then another. "Oh, Yosef, he's coming!" she screams, half crying, half laughing. Her face contorts and she bears down with all her might. "Ahhh. . . " she moans, grunting and groaning.

Yosef braces and positions himself to receive the baby. He bites his lip and reaches out to guide the little head. He spreads his large hands, now quaking violently, but suddenly, all fear fades and he feels encompassed in peace. It's as though God himself has come, giving him strength for the greatest challenge of his life.

Now, with the grace of an angel, he guides this red-faced infant out into the world. Suddenly, a baby's cry splits the midnight air. Then skillfully, like a master craftsman, Yosef carefully ties the umbilical cord, then cuts it.

"He's beautiful, Miryam," Yosef cries, as his trembling hands hold up this tiny, steaming, squirming baby.

A Baby's Cry

Miryam smiles weakly as she looks at his warm, wet little body. Then he cries again, a loud, piercing, powerful wail. Miryam gasps. The baby's cry impales her heart, and she realizes—this is the first time the voice of God has been heard on earth in almost five hundred years.

Yes, now at last the voice of God has rung through Isra'el again. Indeed, he whose cry tumbled galaxies into space, now cries in his mother's arms. He who sprinkled the universe with gleaming stars, now rests in a virgin's embrace. He who gazed into the eyes of his Father God, now gazes into the eyes of a teenage Jewish girl.

A great surge of love flames up in her heart as she pats her face with his hands. She uncovers his tiny feet and presses them to her lips. With tears clinging to her lashes, she looks into his shining liquid eyes, though swollen and half closed from childbirth. Her heart seems to melt into his.

With a heavy sigh, she lifts up her little one to God. "ADONAI, here is your beautiful Son! This is the one who carries your blood rushing through his veins. Who carries your glory flooding through his being. Who carries your power filling his heart. I know you love him even more than Yosef and I do, so please take care of him!"

A Baby's Cry

She smiles to herself, knowing this one in her arms is fully God yet he is also fully man. He hungers, he thirsts, he sleeps, he wets, he weeps like any baby boy. She closes her eyes, exhausted and happy, thinking of the wonder of God in human flesh.

Yes, this is the glory of the Incarnation![47] God himself enfleshed in human skin. The Creator has become a created being. He who filled eternity with his *Sh'khinah* glory, now fills a baby's flesh. The Infinite has become an infant. The Shepherd of Eternity has become a Lamb.

Seven

BEIT-LECHEM'S LAMB

Born to Be Slain in Yerushalayim

The hills outside the slumbering Beit-Lechem lie quiet and still. Shepherds tending their flocks have drifted off to sleep. Except for the occasional bleating of a lamb, the rhythmic chirping of crickets, the crackle of the fire, and the soft gurgle of a nearby stream, all is silent.

Then suddenly—explosions of light flood the skies. The shepherds awake, astonished. Glory inflames the sky, bathing the heavens with brightness. Light showers across the hillside and shimmers down upon the herdsmen and their flocks.

Fear strikes each shepherd's heart. They leap to their feet, rubbing their eyes and trembling, amazed by this supernatural sight. The *Sh'khinah of* A‍DONAI, the very presence of God, charges the atmosphere, enwrapping them with mantles of throbbing light. Their blood races. They dare not speak a word. They can barely breathe.

They look on terrified as the vague form of an angel appears in the midst of the brilliance. With the authority of God, he says:

> Do not be afraid! For behold, I proclaim Good News to you, which will be great joy to all the people. A Savior is born to you today in the city of David, who is Messiah the Lord.[48]

Every man's heart almost stops. They look at one another, unable to speak, dazed and blinking. "A Savior?" they finally murmur among themselves. "The Mashiach (Messiah)?" "Born right here in the town of David, the city of Beit-Lechem?" As they stand there, dumbfounded, the angel continues:

> And the sign to you is this: You will find an infant wrapped in strips of cloth and lying in a manger.[49]

"A manger? A crude animal feeding trough? How strange to put a baby where the flocks feed!" whispers one of the shepherds.

But before he can continue, the skies split open and hosts of angelic beings flood the heavens above them. From horizon to horizon they gather, lighting the skies with rainbows of splendor, shining bright and glorious. With one magnificent crescendo of praise the heavenly hosts shout:

> Glory to God in the highest, and on earth, shalom to men of good will.[50]

Every shepherd falls to his face on the rocky ground, awestruck by God's glory. But then, just as quickly as the angelic host has come, they depart and the heavens close. The shepherds slowly stand, shaken and wondering.

"Why would angels come to us?" they wonder among themselves. "Who are we? We are nobodies. Mere peasants. The poorest of the poor." "Why would an angel bother to tell us about the Savior of the whole world?" they question.

Indeed none of them are scholars of the Bible. None are experts of the Law. They hold no lofty positions. They are the off scouring of humanity, for they merely tend the sheep.

"I think I know why," stammers Moshe, the oldest shepherd among them. ADONAI must have seen our hearts and our longing for the Mashiach, and so he has told us of this great event!"

"Come on, let's get going into Beit-Lechem and find this Mashiach in a manger!" cries a young man. Grabbing their cloaks and staffs, with a few lambs tucked under their arms for gifts, which is all they had to give, they head down the hill into the town. As they approach the city gates, they see the streets jammed with pilgrims.

But how will they ever find one tiny baby in this bustling mass of humanity? From house to house and inn to inn they search. Then suddenly, the youngest shepherd cries, "Look!" Pointing toward the sky, he says, "That brilliant star! See how it hovers over that little hill leading down to the edge of town?"

"Yes, yes!" chimes Moshe. "I noticed a strange bright star while we were out with our flocks in the field. If God would speak to us through an angel, he could surely lead us by a star. Let's follow it!"

The shepherds hasten down the hillside where they see starlight gleaming over a cave. As they near the cave they pause, disappointed. "Oh, it's only an animal stable. This couldn't be the place where a Mashiach would be born. No Savior of the world could rest his head, like us, amidst the filth and stench of sheep!"

Then they remember. The angel said, "And the sign to you is this: You will find an infant wrapped in strips of cloth and lying in a manger."[51] Though this doesn't seem like the proper place for a Mashiach to be born, as shepherds, they know that feeding troughs are found in stables. So in one accord they nod and agree, "This must surely be the place of his birth!"

A deep hush falls over them as they come to the mouth of the cave. They tiptoe toward the opening and peer in, knowing they are about to witness a miracle.

In the silence they hear the braying of a donkey. The bleating of a few sheep. A mouse scurries beneath the hay. And then. . . the cry of a baby. With eyes wide they gaze into the cave. What they see leaves them breathless.

Here he lies, wrapped in rags and cradled in the hay of a manger, just as the angel said. The soft golden light of a low burning fire illumines the cave. A shaft of starlight, streaming through an opening, focuses all of its light on him, causing the swaddling cloths to shine like polished silver.

Yosef sees the look of wonder on their faces, and he motions for them to come inside the cave. Miryam stiffens and reaches for her baby. She holds him close as if to protect him from these crude, smelly, filthy shepherds.

"It's alright, Miryam," Yosef assures her, smiling knowingly. He tenderly takes the baby from Miryam's arms and nestles him in the manger.

Beit-Lechem's Lamb

Miryam looks on, her heart in her throat, as these ruddy, rawboned, wide-eyed shepherds stoop over the manger and gaze upon their Mashiach. In absolute awe, these rough, scraggly-bearded men begin to tremble and weep like babies as they look into the face of God.

She feels a surge of joy mingled with a stabbing pain, as these calloused men shed tears over her baby. For in her heart she knows that Yeshua is not hers alone. He is the Savior of the world — born to be shared with humanity.

Each shepherd kneels, brushing away tears. Their faces burn with the heat of the glory now filling the cave. Though they cannot explain it, they know they are viewing their long-awaited Jewish Mashiach. One by one, those who carry lambs lay them as gifts in front of the make-shift crib.

As the shepherds file slowly out of the cave, Miryam fixes her eyes on the little lambs, nestled at the foot of the manger. Wistfully, as she cuddles her baby near, she thinks how much Yeshua is like these little lambs.

Then a painful thought invades her mind. Sadly she recalls that these little lambs are born for one purpose. Because Beit-Lechem lies less than six miles south of Yerushalayim (Jerusalem), these lambs,

Beit-Lechem's Lamb

which are brought forth in the hills outside the city, are destined to be sacrificed in the temple.

Oh A<small>DONAI</small>, are you trying to tell me something about my son? Is this why you made sure he was born in Beit-Lechem? Out of all the villages, and hamlets, and towns in Isra'el, is this why you chose Beit-Lechem for his birthplace?

No! That cannot be Yeshua's destiny! Surely A<small>DONAI</small> does not want his Son to be sacrificed like a Beit-Lechem lamb?

And yet. . . is this why my son has been born in a stable, a fitting place for a lamb? Is this why he lays his head in an animal feeding trough, a perfect crib for a lamb? And could this be why, out of all the people on earth, lowly shepherds are the first to attend his birth? For shepherds always attend the birth of lambs!

But Yeshua is the Mashiach! He is born to be the King, like his forefather King David, never a Lamb for sacrifice. He is destined to bring your power and glory back to Isra'el! But why are you showing me these things?

She bows her head, her heart trembling with a mother's tender, protective love. *Are you showing me something I don't want to see? Is my son born to become a Lamb? Not just any lamb, but Beit-Lechem's Lamb — born on earth to be slain?*

Eight

BLOODBATH IN BEIT-LECHEM

Miryam's Pierced Heart

An old man shuffles up the narrow cobble stone streets of Yerushalayim, his long white hair flowing in the breeze. Excitement fills his heart and compels him toward the temple mount.

To himself he thinks, *Today I will see the consolation of Isra'el. The Mashiach of* ADONAI. *I know I will see him today! I just know it!*

As Shim'on (Simeon) nears the temple, the white stone columns and gold engravings shine brightly in the morning sunlight. He hobbles up the massive stone steps, feeling an unusual spring in his normally aching limbs.

Bloodbath in Beit-Lechem

Shim'on has waited his whole life for the promise of the Mashiach to be fulfilled. Now at last, in the twilight of his life, the moment for which he has earnestly prayed is here.

He pauses to wash at the mikveh before entering the temple. His heart hammers with heavy strokes as he enters the Court of the Goyim (Gentiles). Here the clamor of money changers, the bleating of lambs and other animals, can be heard, but all he can hear is the thundering of his own heart.

He hastens through the Court of the Women, the cheeks of his face flushing hot with the spirit of revelation. He elbows his way through the crowd, looking, searching, longing.[52]

Then suddenly, he halts, arrested by the *Ruach HaKodesh*. He feels the trembling rising from deep within. His hands shake and his eyes burn like torches. *That's him,* he thinks, spying a young Jewish girl holding a baby on the inner steps.

Yosef and Miryam have brought the child up to Yerushalayim to present him to the Lord, as it is written in the *Torah* of Moshe, "every first born male is to be consecrated to ADONAI."[53]

The law demanded a payment of five shekels to redeem him back. But this was also the time of Miryam's purification, which required, according to

Bloodbath in Beit-Lechem

the *Torah*, a one-year old lamb for a burnt offering or two doves or pigeons if one is poor.[54]

Drops of sweat glisten on Miryam's brow as she stands in the heat holding the baby Yeshua. When the cohen (priest) finally gives the signal, Yosef hands him two pigeons,[55] whose throats he quickly slices, sprinkling their blood upon her and declaring her clean from the contamination of childbirth.[56]

Miryam then hands him five silver shekels to "redeem the firstborn." The cohen pronounces the benediction and she descends the steps.

Smiling and looking up, she whispers under her breath, "Oh, ADONAI, here I am being purified from the birth of your holy Son and paying the 'redemption price' for the Redeemer of Isra'el himself!"

Shim'on (Simeon), the old prophet, stands back reverently, watching and waiting until the purification is completed. He too knows the irony of this situation as the Redeemer himself is redeemed, and the mother is purified from the birth of the pure One.

Then, with his heart still pounding passionately in his chest, he approaches Miryam and reaches out his arms for the child.

Bloodbath in Beit-Lechem

His abruptness startles her. She flinches back, shielding her baby. But when she sees his sparkling eyes and the glory blushing on his face, she knows the *Ruach HaKodesh* is upon him. Darting a glance toward Yosef, she cautiously hands the child to Shim'on.

Lifting him up, the prophet bellows through the temple courts, with a voice as strong as any young man's, his prayer to Yahweh:

> Now, ADONAI, according to your word, your servant is at peace as you let him go; for I have seen with my own eyes your yeshu'ah, which you have prepared in the presence of all peoples—a light that will bring revelation to the *Goyim* (Gentiles) and glory to your people Isra'el.[57]

His words seem to come from a verse in Yesha'Yahu (Isaiah): "I shaped you and made you a covenant for the people, to be a light for the Goyim, so that you can open blind eyes, free the prisoners from confinement, those living in darkness from the dungeon."[58]

But then the old man turns and looks deep into Miryam's eyes. Solemnly he says, "This child will cause many in Isra'el to fall and to rise, he will become a sign whom people will speak against...."

Bloodbath in Beit-Lechem

It's what he said next, that stunned her. "Moreover, a sword will pierce your own heart too. All this will happen in order to reveal many people's inmost thoughts."[59]

Strangely, Miryam can feel these words driving sharp and deep, like the quick thrust of a blade, into her sensitive being.

However, before she can give it any serious reflection, a beautiful, white-haired old woman, named Hannah (Anna) from the tribe of Asher, rushes up to her. With her face glowing like the light of dawn, she carefully pulls the fringes of the blanket and looks into the baby's face. She reels back in ecstatic praise, overjoyed at seeing her Mashiach.

The little family returns to Beit-Lechem, where they temporarily settle down. They long to return to their loved ones in Natzeret, but it is too soon for such a long journey.

One night Yosef works late, fashioning a little bed for Yeshua, who has already outgrown his manger. He pauses to look up and a shower of starlight fills the night skies over Beit-Lechem. He marvels at this one bright star, which hung like a shining globe over the stable on that momentous night of Yeshua's birth.

Bloodbath in Beit-Lechem

The star still shimmers brightly, raining down rays of light over their little hut. The verse from the *Torah* fills his mind: "A star will step forth from Ya'akov."[60] *I wonder if this...*

Suddenly, his thoughts are interrupted by the crunch of heavy hooves coming up the road. He looks out to see a strange procession of camels with lavishly dressed princes astride.

What is this? Who are these strange men on camels, coming up the road? Perhaps they are wealthy merchants or even kings, he thinks, *but what business could they possibly have in this part of Beit-Lechem?*

"Excuse me, Sir," interrupts one of the men. "We are Maji from the far East and we have been following a certain star, looking for the King of the Jews."[61]

"Yes," said another, "We stopped in Yerushalayim where the priests said that according to the Scripture, the Mashiach would be born in 'Beit-Lechem of Y'hudah.'"[62]

Pointing upward he says, "We were overjoyed when we followed the star and found it hovering here over your house.[63] Can you help us, for we have come to behold this Mashiach and King?"

Bloodbath in Beit-Lechem

Yosef's heart leaps to his throat. He stands up tall, clenching his fists. Edging over in front of the door of his house, he takes a protective stance.

"Sir, we have come to bring gifts and to worship the King of the Jews," said another, his eyes bright with hope.

Yosef hesitates, the tension easing. "Let me tell my wife," he says. Quietly opening the door he finds her nursing the baby. "Miryam, some princes from the East have come to see our baby. They have come with gifts to honor the King of the Jews."

"Alright, let them in, Yosef," she says, covering herself. "They must have come from far away and are probably tired and cold."

Yosef steps back out and invites them in. He watches the men, dressed in rich brocades and silks, tapping the necks of their camels. The massive animals fold their legs and crouch as they dismount.

Reverently they enter the little house as the sound of swishing silken robes and the fragrance of exotic perfumes drifts through the humble dwelling.

Yosef looks at them warily, but relaxes when he sees the look on their faces, their shining eyes fixed on the face of the child. One by one the Maji remove their jeweled turbans and fall prostrate on their faces before him. Miryam and Yosef stand amazed.

Bloodbath in Beit-Lechem

Slowly the Maji arise, a hush of reverence on each of them. The first man lays his treasure chest full of gold before the little one. "For the Prince of Glory," he says radiantly, "for he is the King of all kings!"

The next one, swarthier in complexion, places a gem covered jar of rich incense at his feet. "For the One whose fragrance will fill the whole earth."

The last one hesitates, his throat tight with emotion. He gently lays down a vase of liquid myrrh. "For his death," he softly sighs, barely able to speak, "for he has been born to die for a fallen human race!"

Miryam's chest tightens as she hears these words, for she knows that myrrh is used to embalm dead bodies.

"You must leave Beit-Lechem immediately!" warns one of the Maji. "Herod's jealousy has been aroused and he will seek to kill him before his time."

The men quickly depart, mounting their camels and tapping their necks, which signals them to rise from a crouching position. Then they ride off into the night.

Yosef watches, amazed by what he has just seen. Then he realizes, *I must comfort Miryam. She will be beside herself with worry because of this foreboding news.*

Bloodbath in Beit-Lechem

"Oh, Yosef, what did they mean?" shrieks Miryam, her mind swimming with terror. "Our child must be in danger!"

"I don't know, but let's try to get some sleep. The Lord will show us what to do."

That night Yosef awakens, trembling and soaked in sweat. "What's wrong, my Love?" Miryam asks sleepily, sensing his fear. Then she feels his glistening body, wet with perspiration. She sits up abruptly. "What is it, Yosef?" she cries, her voice quivering. "Something must be terribly wrong!"

"Miryam, we must leave immediately, just like the Maji said. In a dream I saw the angel and heard him say, 'Get up. . . take the child and his mother and escape to Egypt, and stay there until I tell you to leave. For Herod is going to look for the child in order to kill him.'"[64]

A muffled scream breaks from Miryam's throat. She falls against Yosef's side, knowing her worst fears are becoming a reality.

"Quickly, Miryam. Our son is in danger! We must gather a few belongings and leave for Egypt now!" Neither of them know that this will ultimately fulfill the verse in the *Tanakh* that says, "Out of Egypt I called my son."[65]

Bloodbath in Beit-Lechem

They rise and leave hurriedly, Yosef leading the donkey with Miryam and the child on the cart. They have gathered only a few possessions, knowing they will probably never return.

Even now, as they head south on a back road to Egypt, they can hear the sound of horses hooves thundering down from Yerushalayim toward Beit-Lechem. Already swords are being drawn for the bloodbath as all Jewish boys under two-years-old will be butchered before the eyes of their own horrified parents.

The grief this night in Beit-Lechem is indescribable, for, as written in the *Tanakh*:

> A voice is heard in Ramah, lamenting and bitter weeping. It is Rachel weeping for her children, refusing to be comforted for her children, because they are no longer alive.[66]

As the little cart hurtles down the road, Miryam's head swims. She presses her little boy closer, soaking him with her tears.

Suddenly, the strange words of Shim'on in the temple flood her mind: "Moreover, a sword will pierce your own heart too."[67] Even now, she can feel the blade of the sword twisting and cutting somewhere deep inside.

Bloodbath in Beit-Lechem

But the pain she feels tonight is not for herself. It is for all the grief stricken mothers in Beit-Lechem. She can almost picture them, weeping furiously, holding their bleeding babies in their arms as life drains out of their little bodies.

An indescribable, aching sorrow fills her, for she knows, these babies are dying in the place of her son.

And she wonders—*Is this bloodbath in Beit-Lechem a fore glimpse of something that looms ahead?*

Nine

"WHERE'S THE LAMB?"
Roasting the Paschal Lamb

The morning sun spills gently over the hills of Y'udah as a festive caravan from Galilee heads south toward Yerushalayim. Miryam and Yosef have finally returned from Egypt to their beloved home in Natzeret, and now they join family and friends to celebrate the feast of Pesach (Passover) in the holy city.[68]

This is Yeshua's first time to visit Yerushalayim since his dedication as a baby. As they tread happily toward the great city, Yeshua, though only twelve, seems blood-earnest about getting there.

When they finally reach the city gates, after four days of travel, a somber quietness falls over him.

When he sees the grandeur of the temple, its polished, snow-white stone and pure gold trappings

"Where's the Lamb?"

gleaming in the morning sunlight, his cheeks redden and his eyes glisten.

The temple rises like a towering palace on the crest of a hill—Mount Moriyah—the place where Avraham offered his sacrifice.

As they climb the massive stone steps, Yeshua remains quiet and pensive. His thoughts fill with passages from the *Torah,* especially the call of God to Avraham: "Take your son, your only son, whom you love, Yitz'chak (Isaac); and go to the land of Moriyah. There you are to offer him as a burnt offering on a mountain that I will point out to you."[69]

Yeshua knows that *Torah* means "instruction," so as he walks, he meditates on the instructive meaning of this story. He pictures the scene as Avraham climbs this same mount with the fire and the dagger in his hand. He imagines Yitz'chak carrying the wood of the burnt offering over his shoulders.

He knows that to prepare a burnt offering, Avraham must slit his son's throat, splash his blood upon an altar, skin him and slice him in pieces, arrange the pieces of his flesh back in the shape of a boy, then set him aflame as a burnt offering.[70]

Yeshua's heart almost caves in at the thought of the grief this must have caused his father. Then he

"Where's the Lamb?"

recalls Yitzchak's stunning question: "My Father. . . I see the fire and the wood, but where is the lamb for the burnt offering?"

This question burns in Yeshua's mind. He feels it resounding and resonating within him. It fills his whole being, causing him to ask what he cannot hold back. He lifts his face to heaven and cries, "Father, where *is* the lamb?"

Then suddenly, he halts on the steps. He closes his eyes as though listening to the Father's voice. His face turns scarlet. He covers his mouth so as not to alarm his mother, then he shouts up to heaven, "Father, am *I* the Lamb?"

"Yeshua, what's wrong?" his mother asks. Though he walks several paces behind her, she still hears his muffled cry. The words strike her to the heart. *Does he know? I've never told him who he is. I wanted him to learn it from the Torah and from ADONAI himself.*

Finally coming to the top of the steps, they enter the Court of the Gentiles (Goyim). Walking into the court where money changers sell animals for sacrifice, a heavy sadness comes over Yeshua, then anger.

The sight is horrifying. Innocent animals bleat and bawl piteously, frantic for their lives. Miryam

"Where's the Lamb?"

doesn't know what Yeshua is thinking, but she always feels his heart.

As they continue to walk through the temple, the heavy aroma of incense and smoke fills the air. White clad cohen (priests) capped in linen turbans swarm through the temple courts, some of them singing from the Tehillim (Psalms) while playing timbrels and lyres.

Yeshua carries over his shoulders his little lamb, which will be slain for their Paschal meal. Miryam watches his face as he hands the lamb to his father.

Tears fill His eyes and his face drains chalk white as he sees Yosef unsheathe a long sharp knife. Yeshua has seen many lambs slain before, but this one is special to him.

The knife flashes, slicing the throat of the innocent lamb, and then a Levite catches the blood in a bowl and slings it in a crimson stream toward the base of the altar.[71] The leftover blood is siphoned into a gutter which empties into the Brook Kidron at the foot of Mount Moriyah.

Yeshua is sick to his stomach. He wretches, hoping no one sees. Then he recovers and quickly helps Yosef slide a pomegranate stave through the body of the lamb "from mouth to vent."[72] They lift

"Where's the Lamb?"

the lamb on the pole and carry it to Elisheva and Z'kharyah's (Zechariah's) home near the city, where it will be roasted for the Passover meal.

Later that afternoon, Miryam finds Yeshua in the courtyard, watching the lamb roasting over the flames. The fat of the lamb drips down hissing on the coals.

"What are you thinking?" She asks.

He doesn't answer, but she knows. This was his own precious lamb, but she suspects his thoughts go even deeper.

That night, amidst flickering candle light, servants place a bottle of red wine, a platter of unleavened bread, bitter herbs, and roasted lamb on the table.

Yeshua remains subdued, absorbed in his thoughts. He thinks again of the passages from the *Torah* concerning the Paschal lamb, primarily the words ADONAI spoke long ago to Moshe:

> You are to keep it (a lamb) until the fourteenth day of the month, and then the entire assembly of the community of Isra'el will slaughter it at dusk. They are to take some of the blood and smear it on the two sides and top of the door-

"Where's the Lamb?"

frame at the entrance of the house in which they eat it.

Yeshuah's heart races when he thinks of the next words:

> That night, they are to eat the meat, roasted in the fire; they are to eat it with *matzah* and *maror*. Don't eat it raw or boiled, but roasted in fire, with its head, the lower parts of its legs and its inner organs. Let nothing remain, burn it up completely.[73]

Of course, every Jewish person knows that Pesach commemorates the night in Egypt when the death angel passed over the homes. Wherever the doorposts were splattered with lamb's blood, the firstborn son was saved.

But this night, as the family eats the lamb, Yeshua barely touches it. He seems to be seeing more than history past. Lost in thought, he seems to be seeing history future in this eating of the Paschal lamb.[74]

Again Yitz'chak's question haunts him, "Father, . . . where is the lamb?" He maintains his composure, but simmering in his mind burns the thought— *"Father, am I the Lamb?"*

"Where's the Lamb?"

Z'kharyah pours the cups of wine and both Elisheva and Miryam notice how his hand shakes and his eyes rim with tears. He is very old, but not too old to remember who Yeshua is.

When he comes to the part of the meal in which he lifts up three pieces of matzah bread, his hand shakes more violently. These three pieces of unleavened bread speak of Avraham, Yitz'chak, and Ya'akov (Jacob), but Z'kharyah reaches in, pulls out Yitz'chak (Isaac), and breaks it. Yeshua puts his head down and covers his face.

Finally, the meal ends with the singing of the Hallel (Psalms 113-118). When they come to the words in the song, "The very rock that the builders rejected has become the cornerstone," Yeshua lifts his head and looks at his mother. His eyes are moist and red. His heart is in his eyes.

A few days later the group of happy Nazarenes, leave the city to travel the long distance back to Natzeret.

The young boys run ahead of the caravan, and Miryam assumes that Yeshua is with them. Soon they cross over the Yarden River and head north along the shining waters.

As they tramp the dusty road, the landscape begins to change from rugged hills to vast green fields

"Where's the Lamb?"

and terraces, splashed with colorful spring flowers. Yellow field lilies and crimson colored anemones sprinkle the fields like flecks of shining gold encrusted with blood red rubies.

Miryam takes in the scenery, breathing in the fresh spring air and the fragrance of lemon and orange blossoms. Her heart swells with thoughts of how much she loves Galilee with its rolling pastures, dotted with grazing sheep, its rich vineyards, and glistening lakes.

Suddenly, one of her nephews runs up and breathlessly cries, "Have you seen Yeshua? We can't find him anywhere!"

Miryam's stomach lurches. "What?" Fear clenches her throat. "I thought he was with you!"

In the excitement from the feast, no one noticed that Yeshua stayed behind. "Oh, Yosef, we must find him!" she cries, almost hysterical with fear.

Ever since the bloodbath in Beit-Lechem when Herod, intent on killing the Mashiach, slaughtered every baby boy under two years of age, she has feared for his life.[75] There on a back road from Beit-Lechem, as they escaped to Egypt, she had released him to the Father, but as his mother, she still feels the need to protect him.

"Where's the Lamb?"

Yet somehow, in the flush of joy which filled her as they left Yerushalayim, she assumed he was with his cousins. Now they frantically search the throng of people, but no one has seen him.

With her heart in her throat, Miryam says, "Yosef, I think he will be back in the temple. Let's turn back and find him."

"Yes, yes. I agree," says Yosef. Together they head back down the road toward the city.

"Oh, Yosef, do you think he knows? In a way I think he has always suspected, but this trip to the temple has awakened something deep within him. Could he know that he is the Mashiach?"

"We must hurry, my Love, for already darkness has fallen. If we press through the night, we can get to Jerushalayim in time for the gates to open in the morning." Miryam's feet ache and her head pounds but the fierceness of love rushes her onward.

As the sun begins to paint the sky with tinges of orange, they reach the temple, exhausted and worried. Hastening up the stone steps they enter the massive gate and scan the Court of the Women. Desperately they search through the colonnades and porches, but the courts throng with people, still lingering from the feast. Yeshua is nowhere to be found. All day they search, but to no avail.

"Where's the Lamb?"

Finally, on the third day, they peek inside the court of the cohanim (priests). Here sits Yeshua, among the rabbis and doctors of the Law. Miryam breathes a sigh of relief and leans against Yosef. Quietly they stand, listening to Yeshua as he plies the priests with questions. Because it is Pesach, he seems to be probing them with questions about the Pascal lamb.

Miryam strains to hear. Something about spotless male lambs. . . blood spilled out at the altar. . . none of its bones broken. . . the lamb lifted up on a wooden pole. . . only roasted in fire, never baked or boiled.

The priests give their standard answers from the *Torah* and tradition. But Yeshua, his face aglow with the spirit of revelation, begins explaining to them the answers.

"Have you not read?" he asks, his eyes twinkling. Then he tells them how the Mashiach will fulfill every detail of the Passover lamb. As he speaks, though he is only twelve, his words burn with truth and power.

When Miryam hears this, her knees weaken. The scribes and Pharisees stand listening, some baffled, some incensed with anger, and some enthralled.

"*Where's the Lamb?*"

A man named Nakdimon (Nicodemus) and an older one named Yosef, seem awestruck by the brilliance of truth coming from the lips of this boy.

Others snarl, "Who does he think he is, telling us—the doctors of the Law—the meaning of the Paschal lamb?"

Suddenly, Yeshua looks up and sees his mother. He smiles broadly, but when he sees her dark, scowling face, he halts his dialogue.

Her brow is furrowed, her face flushed with worry. He quietly dismisses himself and slips through the crowd to join her and Yosef.

"Son, why have you treated us like this? Your father and I have been searching for you everywhere.[76] We've been beside ourselves with worry, thinking we had lost you!"

Looking at her with pleading eyes, he says, "Eema (Mama), 'didn't you know that I had to be concerning myself with my Father's affairs?'"[77]

She doesn't respond. She only looks at him with sadness in her eyes.

Threading their way through the crowd in the courtyard, they silently descend the long stone steps leading down from the temple mount. Yeshua pauses on the steps and asks, "Eema (Mama), do you

"Where's the Lamb?"

understand what I've been feeling here in the temple in Yerushalayim?"

"Yes, Son, I think I do."

"As I climbed these steps up Mount Moriyah, I kept thinking of Avraham, called by A<small>DONAI</small> to offer his son as a burnt offering. Over and over again, I kept hearing Yitz'chak's question, 'Father, where is the lamb?' And Avraham's response, 'God will provide *himself* a lamb.'"

Miryam nods.

"Then I watched my little lamb, pouring out his blood on the altar in the temple." Tears fill Yeshua's eyes as he tries to express his heart. "And I stood in the courtyard watching my lamb roasting over the flames."

Her throat tightens.

Yeshua turns and looks deeply into Miryam's eyes. For a moment their eyes lock. Finally he asks, "Only you my mother could know... Eema, am I born to become the Pascal Lamb? Even more, am I destined to become the fulfillment of *Avraham's Lamb?*"

His question impales her heart. She closes her eyes, leans against Yosef, and whispers raggedly—"He knows."

SECTION THREE

The Seed of Avraham's Lamb Dies

In the northern regions of Isra'el, the River Yarden (Jordan) runs wild and cold this time of year. It rushes in foaming torrents from Mount Hermon's melting snows and empties into the teeming waters of Lake Kinneret (the Sea of Galilee).

As the river streams down from the Kinneret (Sea of Galilee), it meanders past Yericho (Jericho), where a young man stands immersing Jewish people in the chilly waters. The rugged young man burns with a passion to prepare the way for Isra'el's Mashiach...

Ten

"BEHOLD THE LAMB"

Is the Mashiach a King or a Lamb?

The river sparkles in the morning sunlight, splashing around rocks and twisting its way through the land, bringing life wherever it flows.

A breeze blows up fresh and cool from the waters. Yochanan the Immerser (John the Baptist), son of Elisheva and Z'kharyah, stands in the midst of the river, immersing all who will repent of their sins.

Suddenly, Yochanan stops his immersing and looks up. His face beams brightly when he sees him coming.

It's his own distant Jewish cousin, Yeshua bar Yosef, coming to him to be immersed. The Immerser feels entirely unqualified, but as he slowly lowers him into the water, his arms trembling, something amazing happens.

"Behold the Lamb"

Suddenly, the heavens above tear open and the *Ruach HaKodesh* descends upon him like a dove.[78] Then a voice from heaven roars, *"You are my Son, whom I love, I am well pleased with you."*[79]

A sudden stillness falls over the entire multitude which has gathered at the river, stunned by this rumble of the heavens above them.

Moments pass. Finally, Yochanan, breaks the silence. Taking a deep breath, he lifts up his arm and points directly at Yeshua. With passion blazing in his voice, he thunders—"BEHOLD THE LAMB OF GOD, who takes away the sin of the world!"[80]

His words strike like bolts of lightning into the hearts of the people. "The Lamb?" "What is the Immerser saying?" "Is he telling us that this man, this carpenter's son, is the fulfillment of all the lambs which have been slaughtered in Isra'el through the centuries?"

These questions ripple through the people who are gathered at the river. "Is he saying that this young Nazarene is the fulfillment of Avraham's sacrifice on Mount Moriyah?[81] Is he the completion of Moshe's Paschal lamb and the hundreds of thousands of lambs slain at Passover?"[82]

"Is the Immerser saying that he fulfills the millions more lambs slain twice daily for over fifteen

"Behold the Lamb"

hundred years as burnt offerings?" They turn to one another, mumbling their bewilderment. "How can this carpenter's son from Natzeret be the fulfillment of all these lambs?"

The next day, the Immerser's talmidim (disciples), Andrew and another young man named Yochanan (John), stand with him talking. Yeshua walks by and the Immerser again cries, "Behold the Lamb of God!"

When the two talmidim hear these words, they drop everything and follow Yeshua.

For a brief time Yeshua slips off into the wilderness, but when he returns, he is bursting with anointing for ministry. He gathers his talmidim (disciples) and sets out to spread his kingdom through the land.

In the months that follow Miryam stays in the background, yet always grasping for any bit of news she can hear about her son.

All over the Galil (Galilee) people are buzzing with rumors about him, telling of the amazing miracles and signs and wonders. How she longs to be with him, but she knows his time has come and she must stay out of the way.

"Behold the Lamb"

One day, a few years later, Miryam, who is now a widow, takes her children and her mother to visit the home of her sister, Shlomit (Salome) and Zavdai (Zebedee). As they sit around a fire, sharing memories, suddenly Zavdai bursts through the door and announces, "Look who's here!"

Yochanan (John the Beloved) and his older brother Ya'akov (James) peep around the door, smiling broadly. They are now part of the talmidim (disciples) who follow Yeshua, and they have been out ministering with him for over two years. The children squeal and everyone jumps to their feet, surrounding them with hugs. Miriyim waits, shaken, desperate to hear the latest news of her son.

The brothers brim with excitement, but when Yochanan the Beloved sees Miryam, he rushes to her side and kneels down beside her. "Let me tell you how it all began," he says warmly, knowing she will want to hear.

"I was following Elisheva's son Yochanan the Immerser, when one day he pointed at Yeshua and proclaimed, 'Behold the Lamb of God!'[83] My heart leapt and I knew I must follow him for the rest of my life!"

Miryam's face pales. With a tremor in her voice, she asks softly, "Did I hear you say the

"Behold the Lamb"

Immerser announced that Yeshua is the Lamb of God?"

"Oh yes! It was powerful. The Immerser lifted his voice and exploded the words like an erupting volcano. I had never heard him speak with such thunderous, prophetic authority."

Miryam closes her eyes and a tear starts down her cheek. She has held this secret in her heart for so long. She recalls again his birth in Beit-Lechem, where lambs are born to be slain. She thinks of the animal stable with only a feeding trough to lay his head. She thinks of the shepherds who were the first to visit the birth of her son, for shepherds always attend the birth of lambs.

She remembers Yeshua's first visit to the temple in Yerushalayim. She can still feel the emotion-charged silence when he saw his precious lamb slaughtered, then watched it roasting for the Paschal meal. Her heart aches as she recalls Yeshua's stunning question while descending the temple steps. Deep into her eyes he had looked. Then he asked, "Only you my mother could know. . . Eema, am I born to become the Lamb?"

She wipes away tears as a verse from the *Tanakh* floods her mind: "Like a lamb led to be slaughtered, like a sheep silent before its shearers, he did not open his mouth."[84]

"Behold the Lamb"

Even now, she can still feel the sharp thrust of an unseen sword, which the prophet had warned her about thirty years ago. Now the pieces fit together as never before and she understands why Yochanan the Immerser (John the Baptist) has called him "the Lamb of God."

But she holds these thoughts to herself, choking back the emotion she feels. Quietly she listens to the brothers, who are her nephews, as they exude with joy about all they have witnessed with Yeshua.

Eagerly, Ya'akov (James) tells about the miracles of the multiplied bread, the raising of a child from the dead, and the hundreds who are healed in Yeshua's meetings.

"Oh, I tell you," cries Yochanan, "Yeshua looks out over crowds and his heart yearns with compassion. Then he reaches out and touches the oozing sores of lepers and the empty sockets of blind men, and they are healed!"

Miryam smiles faintly, for she has always been aware of his love for hurting people. Simply to look into his eyes is to look into the face of love. His eyes are like deep pools, reflecting the mercy and compassion of God.

"Behold the Lamb"

She knows that, though he came from heaven where no tears exist, he has come to his people in human flesh so he could know the feeling of a tear slipping down his cheek.

"And his teachings!" says Ya'akov, "They are transforming. He seems to know the *Torah* by heart, and he opens its meaning in depths we never understood before. He rejects the traditions of men, but he honors the *Torah* and its teachings.

"Yeshua said, 'Don't think that I have come to abolish the *Torah* or the Prophets. I have come not to abolish but to complete. Yes indeed! I tell you that until heaven and earth pass away, not so much as a *yud* or a stroke will pass from the *Torah* — not until everything that must happen has happened.'"[85]

Zavdai (Zebedee) rises and stirs the fire. It crackles and brightens the room. Shlomit (Salome) slips to the kitchen area and Miryam follows her. They return bearing trays of fig cakes and honey, almonds, dates, and mugs of hot apple juice.

"Let me tell you all about the most glorious sight I have ever seen in my life," says Yochanan eagerly, his face lighting up like the fire in the hearth. Everyone leans forward, even the children though they are sleepy from a long trip.

"Behold the Lamb"

"It was almost midnight one night as Yeshua led Kefa (Peter) and Ya'akov (James) and myself up a high mountain to pray. Patches of moon-washed snow dotted the mountainside as we climbed.

Finally, Yeshua stopped and lifted his face to pray. Suddenly. . . " Yochanan's voice rises, trembling with emotion, "Suddenly, Yeshua began to *shine!*"

Miryam's heart beats hard. She can picture everything Yochanan describes. His story brings back, with a thud, the true divinity of her son. She can feel the heat of God's presence burning on the cheeks of her face as the young talmid talks. It is almost as though Yeshua is with them, his presence in the room is so tangible.

"I rubbed my eyes," he continues. "Yeshua glowed as bright as the sunlight. I was awestruck. I could feel the light flooding out from within him. His face glowed with the light of Eternity. So thick was the *Sh'kinah* that I could hardly breathe. It was like heaven had come down to earth."

Yochanan takes in a deep breath and continues. "It was as though the *Sh'khinah,* which once shimmered behind the veil and rested over the ark, could no longer be contained by the veil of Yeshua's body. Like light streaming out of a lantern, the glory of God streamed out from his human flesh.

"Behold the Lamb"

"Oh, Miryam," he cries, looking at her with deepest love and respect. "I have heard Yeshua teach; I've seen him walk on water; I've seen him heal blind eyes, and raise the dead. But as I saw Yeshua shining in his own innate glory there on the mount, I knew that he is God. If I ever doubted, I could never doubt again. 'I saw his *Sh'khinah*, the *Sh'khinah* of the Father's only Son, full of grace and truth.'"[86]

Miryam can hardly contain her emotion as she hears this amazing story of her son's inner glory. Her thoughts race back to a little rooftop terrace in Natzeret, when ADONAI came, like a shining cloud, and covered her with his *Sh'khinah*.

She recalls the explosions of glory that flooded the skies over Beit-Lechem when the *Sh'khinah* appeared above the shepherds and led them to the Lamb. It was all too holy to even speak of, and even now, she holds it to herself. She simply trembles in silence as the tears slip silently down her cheeks.

"But oh, we almost forgot to tell you the most important part," says Ya'akov, stumbling over his words. "It was incredible! With our own eyes we saw Moshe and Eliyahu (Elijah) appear, speaking to him on the mount.

"We were absolutely undone by this sight of these two great Hebrew men, one who brought us the Law and wrote the *Torah*, the other who called down

"Behold the Lamb"

fire on the burnt offering. We could hardly believe our eyes!"

Miryam interrupts. "You say they were talking to him. Could you hear the conversation?"

"Yes. 'They appeared in glorious splendor and spoke to him of his exodus (departure), which he was soon to accomplish in Yerushalayim,'[87] but we didn't know what they meant."

A choked little cry breaks from Miryam's lips. She doesn't speak. She cannot, her heart convulses within her as she thinks of what this means. Everyone turns their eyes toward her, waiting for her to say what she is thinking. Finally, with emotion trembling through her words, she manages to ask, *"His exodus? Soon? In Yerushalayim?"*

"Don't you see?" she continues, her voice quivering. "Yerushalayim is where lambs, which are born in Beit-Lechem, are taken to be slain. Yerushalayim is the place where thousands of Moshe's Paschal lambs are slaughtered. Yes, right there on the rock on Mount Moriyah in Yerushalayim is where our great Patriarch, Avraham, father of our Hebrew nation, sacrificed his lamb."

Each family member looks at her curiously. Miryam swallows hard against the thickness in her

"Behold the Lamb"

throat. "And now Yochanan the Immerser has confirmed the truth that Yeshua is the Lamb of God."

Her voice lowers now to a whisper. "My precious family, it is time for you to know. . . I think you already realize that Yeshua is the long awaited Jewish Mashiach." She pauses and watches their expressions, all of them nodding reverently, tears filling every eye.

"But I must tell you," she says, choking back the emotion, "we have all been expecting a Mashiach who would overthrow the Roman empire and become a magnificent king. We have expected a mighty warrior like King David and a splendid monarch like King Shlomo (Solomon).

She hesitates, her whole body shuddering, "But you need to know— Yeshua is the Mashiach who will lay down his life as a Lamb."

"You see, this is the divine secret hidden since the days of our father Avraham. He is the answer to the ageless question, asked by Yitz'chak long ago: 'Father, where is the lamb?'

"Now, my dear family, the secret is uncovered. The revelation is disclosed. Yeshua is God's Son who will lay down his life as a Lamb. He is the fulfillment of *Avraham's Lamb.*"

Eleven

ADONAI'S CUP

The Second Seder Cup of Judgment

Yochanan, the young talmid (disciple), stumbles through the front door of Elisheva's mountain home outside Yerushalayim. Here Miryam is visiting her elderly cousin for Pesach.

Though well past midnight, he breathlessly cries, "I must tell you what happened tonight! Oh, Miryam, I am heartsick to tell you this..."

Calmly, Yeshua's mother bids him to sit down and tell his story.

"The candles were already lit and the Pascal meal spread out, as we all reclined around the table with Yeshua. He looked at us solemnly and said, 'I have really wanted so much to celebrate this *Seder* with you before I die!'[88]

"*Die?* We were stunned!"

ADONAI'S Cup

Miryam's face drains as she listens.

"Yeshua poured wine mixed with warm water into the first cup, the Cup of Sanctification. As he passed it around, I could feel the thick presence of glory in the room as though the *Sh'khinah* were hovering over us.

"But when he poured the second cup — the Cup of Judgment, something heavy came over him. Yeshua looked long and deep into this cup as though it held some profound meaning for him. His face darkened and I could see a look of pain in his eyes.

"Finally, he led us in dipping a finger into the cup until ten drops had been spilled out into a dish, commemorating the ten plagues in Egypt. Then we drank it and ate the Paschal meal."

The young talmid seems puzzled. "When we finished, he reached into a stack of three pieces of matzos bread, drawing out the middle one. At the time I thought of Avraham, Yitz'chak (Isaac), and Ya'akov (Jacob), but he took out the middle one — Yitz'chak!

"Then he gave the b'rakhah (blessing), broke it, gave it to us and said, 'Take! Eat! This is my body!' Oh, Miryam, what did he mean? Why did he take out Yitz'chak and why did he break it and say it represents his own body? I wanted to ask but I dared not interrupt."

Miryam's thoughts slip back once again to the story of Yitz'chak himself, offered by Avraham on the mount...

But the young talmid continues. "So I just watched with my heart in my throat as he poured wine into the third cup—the Cup of Redemption. He lifted it up, gave the b'rakhah (blessing), and said, 'All of you drink from it! For this is my blood which ratifies the New Covenant, my blood shed on behalf of many, so that they may have their sins forgiven.'[89]

"*His blood?*" Taking in a deep breath, he cries, "What was he saying? My insides were screaming, but I still didn't dare say a word.

Finally, we drank from the fourth cup—the Cup of Elijah or the Kingdom— and he said, 'I tell you, I will not drink this fruit of the vine again until the day I drink new wine with you in my Father's Kingdom.'[90]

"Dear Miryam, do you know what all this means?"

She slowly nods. "Yes, I think I do. I believe Yeshua was interpreting Pesach, just as he did long ago with the doctors of the Law in the temple. I think he was showing you how the Passover speaks of the Mashiach and is fulfilled in him."

Sighing heavily and biting back tears, Yochanan begins now to tell the most painful part of the story. "After this, Yeshua led us out of the city, up the winding, rocky road of the Mount of Olives. He took us to his favorite garden, Gat-Sh'manim (Gethsemane), but such a morbid grief seemed to settle over him that I knew something was terribly, terribly wrong.

"When we entered the garden, laved by moonlight from the full Paschal moon, he said with deep emotion, 'My heart is so filled with sadness that I could die! Remain here and stay awake with me.'[91] His words stabbed me to the heart."

Yochanan pauses to swallow hard and gather his thoughts. "I watched as Yeshua stepped forward about a stone's toss ahead of us, and threw himself on the ground. I slipped up as close as I dared and listened, my heart pounding hard. Then he began to pray, to cry out to God in loud crying and tears of sorrow. I could hardly understand his words, they were filled with such groaning and wailing.

"So I crept up even closer and what I saw knocked the wind from my lungs. Yeshua was writhing on the ground, covered in something dark and wet. I squinted my eyes and saw that his garments were soaked, not merely with sweat, but they were saturated with his own *blood!* It was oozing out of the pores of his skin and falling in large droplets to the ground. I have never in my whole life seen anything like it," he stammers.

The young disciple sees the color rising in Miryam's face as she ponders his story. Everything in her wants to shriek and run out in the night to find her bleeding son, to save him from this impending danger. But she knows she cannot interfere with God's plan, so she tightens her jaw and forces herself to keep listening to the young talmid.

"I don't understand," cries Yochanan, his voice cracking. "But then I heard his prayer and it struck me to my soul. Yeshua prayed, 'O God, take this cup from me!' Over and over again he prayed about this cup.

"What did it mean, Miryam? I have never seen him like this. Here he was—covered in his own clotted blood[92]—praying desperately about some mysterious cup. I didn't understand. But somehow, vaguely, I had the feeling that the second Seder cup from the Passover—the Cup of Iniquity and Judgment—was still on his mind."

Miryam nods slowly, her cheeks crimson. "I think you are right, Yochanan." She closes her eyes as

ADONAI'S Cup

verses from the *Tanakh,* which define this cup, flood her thoughts.

Softly she whispers, "For here is what ADONAI, the God of Isra'el says to me, 'Take this CUP of the wine of my fury from my hand. . . .'"[93] Moments pass. She murmurs again, "In ADONAI'S hand there is a CUP of wine, foaming, richly spiced; when he pours it out, all the wicked of the earth will drain it, drinking it to the dregs."[94]

She pauses and sighs, "You drank the CUP of his fury; you have drained to the dregs, the goblet of drunkenness."[95] "Behold I have taken from your hand the cup of reeling, the bowl of my wrath."[96]

Oh, ADONAI, what does this mean? she silently prays. *Is this the meaning of the second Seder cup in the Pascal meal? Is Yeshua born to drink your cup of iniquity and judgment for sin?*

She can feel the heat of revelation burning on her face as suddenly she remembers Avraham, climbing up the mount. He grasps the dagger in one hand and a cup of fire in the other. *A cup of fire? Yes, he could not have carried raw fire in his bare hand. He would have conveyed it in some kind of cup or bowl.*

Again she closes her eyes and silently prays, *Is this why Avraham carried the fire up the mount? Even as the Tanakh defines this cup as being full of God's wrath, is*

ADONAI'S Cup

this cup of fire in Avraham's hand a shadow of your wrath and judgment? Is this Yeshua's destiny — to bear your wrath and punishment for sin?

Her cheeks burn with the heat and the horror of this vivid revelation. She covers her face and quietly sobs. A long silence follows.

Finally, she lifts her tear stained face and groans, "I have known my son must give his life as a Lamb, but I knew nothing of ADONAI'S *cup!* This must be what the prophet Yesha 'Yahu (Isaiah) meant in the *Tanakh* when he said:

> We regarded him as punished, stricken and afflicted by God. But he was wounded because of our crimes, crushed because of our sins; the disciplining that makes us whole fell on him and by his bruises we are healed.[97]

"This must also be what Yochanan the Immerser (John the Baptist) meant when you heard him cry, 'Behold the Lamb of God who *takes away the sin of the world!*'"

Yochanan nods.

Miryam's whole body begins quietly shaking. She lifts her eyes heavenward and blurts, "Oh ADONAI, this is too much for me to bear! Was my own son—

ADONAI'S Cup

God's innocent Lamb—born to carry away humanity's sin by being punished in our place?"

Yochanan lowers his voice and whispers sadly, "This must be why Yeshua sweated those great clots of blood when he looked into ADONAI'S cup in the garden! This must be why he was writhing on the ground and pleading with God to remove this gruesome cup?

"And I must tell you," he says thickly, "finally I heard him cry out to God, 'Not my will, Abba, but let your will be done.' He bowed his head and seemed to relinquish everything to God.

"But oh, Miryam, how could he do it? Why would he do it? I don't understand!"

Miryam closes her eyes and covers her face with her hands. Within herself she wails the same question. *Oh, Yeshua, my son, how could you do it? How could you surrender yourself to ADONAI'S cup of wrath? How could you be willing to drink the fire of Avraham's cup?*

She waits, then whispers, "Yochanan, all I know is this—Yeshua is compelled by love. He must have looked into ADONAI'S cup there in the garden, and he surely saw what would happen to all of us if he refused to drink it."

ADONAI'S Cup

Yochanan grimaces and says, "Miryam, I must tell you what happened next. Suddenly, Y'hudah (Judas) — *that traitor* — came tearing into the garden with the temple guards. He sauntered right up to Yeshua and planted a kiss on the Master's cheek."

With a faraway look in her eyes, Miryam murmers, "Just as the *Tanakh*, says, 'Even my close friend, on whom I relied, who shared my table, has turned against me.'"[98]

"I was furious," continues the disciple, "and Kefa (Peter) whipped out a sword, wounding one of the men. Yeshua frowned and said, "Put your sword back where it belongs, for everyone who uses the sword will die by the sword. Don't you know that I could ask my Father, and he will instantly provide more than a dozen armies of angels to help me? But if I did that, how could the passages in the *Tanakh* be fulfilled that say it has to happen this way?"[99]

"Then Yeshua looked deep into Kefa's eyes and said firmly, *'This is the cup the Father has given me: am I not to drink it?'*[100]

"Before I had time to think, the temple guards grabbed Yeshua, bound his hands, and forced him off to the cohen gadol's (high priest's) house.

"And then, like cringing cowards, we all scattered and ran away to safety. It was just as

Yeshua had warned us, 'Tonight you will all lose faith in me, as the *Tanakh* says, 'I will strike the shepherd dead, and the sheep of the flock will be scattered.'[101]

"But, Miryam, though I was afraid, I couldn't leave my Master. So I followed from afar and slipped into the temple courtyard. I could hear the priests shouting at him, striking him and mocking him. When he came out, his cheeks were bruised and swollen, chains hung from his wrists, his haggard eyes were sunken and filled with sadness. Patches of his beard were torn from his cheeks and human spittle ran down his face."

Sadly she moans, "For it is written in the *Tanakh,* 'I offered... my cheeks to those who plucked out my beard; I did not hide my face from insult and spitting.'"[102]

"The temple guards then shoved him out of the court and took him to Pilate, accusing him of blasphemy. But I knew I couldn't wait any longer to come to you. You are his mother and I knew I must come and tell you before... before it is too late."

"Oh Yochanan, I must go to him! I cannot let my son endure this agony without his mother near. Please take me to him."

The young disciple nods and motions for her to follow.

Twelve

PREPARING THE BURNT OFFERING
The Meaning of the Holocaust Offering

Miryam and Yochanan rush down the mountainside and up the hill toward the city. The first blush of dawn has risen over the hills of Yerushalayim, and the gates are opening.

Through the narrow, cobbled streets they run, toward the Roman Praetorium. When they come to the Pavement, they see a swelling crowd of Jewish onlookers. *Strange that they should gather so early in the morning*, thinks Miryam.

Sympathetic groans rise from the people in the crowd as they respond to the cruel scourging of a fellow Jew. Her heart sinks when she hears the crack of the whip and the moan of the prisoner. She knows it is the sigh of her son.

Preparing the Burnt Offering

Holding Miryam's hand, Yochanan shoves his way through the mass of people. When they reach the front, and she sees her son tied to a post and standing in a pool of his own blood, she almost faints.

The young disciple holds her as she watches the cruel Roman swing the lash with all his might, slicing Yeshua's body to pieces. It is just as the prophet said, *"I offered my back to those who struck me."*[103]

The Roman scourge, called the flagellum, had long leather strips, studded with pieces of sharp bone and metal, heavily weighted with lead pellets. It could quite literally tear a man's back to bits, shredding him like ground meat.

When finally the thirty-nine lashes have been administered, a soldier unties Yeshua's hands. He slumps to the pavement in a bloody heap. Then the centurion, howling in laughter, rips a purple cloak from one of the soldiers.

"They say this pitiful creature is a king. So here, King of the Jews, put on this royal robe!" He thrusts the robe over his shoulders and jams a rod into his hand.

Another soldier weaves a thorn branch into a crown. They crush it into his head and savagely beat the thorns into his skull and face, for the *Tanakh* says,

Preparing the Burnt Offering

"They are striking the judge of Isra'el on the cheek with a stick."[104] With blood dripping into his eyes, they bow down and hoot, "Hail, King of the Jews!"[105]

The little mother feels nauseated by the sight of her mutilated son. He was almost unrecognizable as a man, as the *Tanakh* says, "His appearance was disfigured more than any man. His form more than the sons of men."[106]

She shuts her eyes and falls helplessly into Yochanan's arms, convulsing in sobs.

Finally, she lifts her eyes to heaven and cries, "Oh, ADONAI, my Abba, I am so sorry that you have to look upon such a hideous violation of your precious gift to the world! I grieve for myself, but I grieve even more for what you must feel."

Yet somehow she knows, this is all part of HaShem's great plan to save his people and draw them close to him. Her thoughts return to Avraham, whose own heart would have ached within him as he prepared to sacrifice his son as a burnt offering on the mount.

For a moment, she ponders again this burnt offering, and then she suddenly knows why Yeshua must endure this cruel scourging. He is being prepared for sacrifice as the morning burnt offering.

Preparing the Burnt Offering

Even as a male lamb is examined for defects by the priests before dawn, he has been examined by the priests before dawn and found to be perfectly flawless.[107] And then, even as the lamb for the burnt offering had to be "cut up in pieces,"[108] Yeshua has been cut into pieces with a scourge, like a lamb for sacrifice.

Miryam turns her face toward the temple and thinks, *Even now the priests will be cutting the lamb into pieces for the morning burnt offering.* Then suddenly, an image of a cut up lamb with flames leaping from its flesh, fills her mind. She sees again Avraham's ram burning on the altar on Moriyah. She tries to push the image away, but it won't leave.

Her heart shakes as she remembers a profound truth her father once taught her about the burnt offering. He explained to her that the highest kind of offering is the whole burnt offering. The word "whole" is *holo* and "burnt" is *caust*. That's why the whole burnt offering is actually called the *holocaust offering*.

Miryam shudders as she realizes what God was telling Avraham to do. He was telling him to offer his own son Yitz'chak as a *holocaust offering!*

Oh no! she thinks, covering her mouth with her hand. She remembers Yeshua's prayer in the Garden of Gat-Sh'manim (Gethsemane), which Yochanan had

Preparing the Burnt Offering

described. His prayer was about a trembling cup, ADONAI'S cup of wrath.

Oh Abba, is this what you have been leading up to? Is this your divine plan? Is my son—your innocent Lamb—destined for this purpose? Is the Son of God preordained to drink the cup of ADONAI and become a Holocaust Lamb?[109]

How could you do it, Abba? How could you give so deeply? How could you love so infinitely? I don't think I will ever fully understand.

She bows her head, trembling. Tears splash her cheeks as she whimpers, "But nevertheless, as my son has prayed in the garden, 'Let your will be done.'"

When the Roman soldiers' sport finally ends, they march Yeshua back to Pilate where a multitude has gathered in the courtyard. When the people see this disfigured man, bleeding like a wounded lamb, many turn away from the grisly sight, for he is "Like someone from whom people turn their faces."[110]

And though he stands, bleeding from every wound in his body, the crowd shows no mercy. "Crucify him! Crucify him!" roars the multitude. Their cry strikes like blows from an unseen sword, driving deep into Miryam's heart.

Preparing the Burnt Offering

"No!" she screams. "He is our Mashiach!" Others around her, join in the cry, "He is our Jewish Mashiach!" Solitary voices shout, "He is a good man!" "He is innocent!" But the raving crowd continues to chant, "Crucify! Crucify!"

Miryam's stomach drops as she looks up and sees a Roman centurion strapping a wooden beam over Yeshua's shoulders. As she watches him stumble out the gate and up the hill, carrying the wood on his back, her heart stands still.

She recalls another scene long ago when Yitz'chak carried the wood on his back as he climbed up the hill of Mount Moriyah. Now the Son of God is trudging up that mountain range outside Yerushalayim, carrying on his back the wood for the sacrifice.[111]

Finally, the grim procession reaches the top of the hill, and the centurion orders Yeshua to be cast down on the slab of wood.

Miryam groans. She knows that at that very moment, the third hour of the morning, a cohen in the temple will be casting the pieces of lamb's meat down on the altar for the morning burnt offering.[112] She turns her gaze toward the temple and watches the smoke of the burnt offering slowly ascending heavenward.

Preparing the Burnt Offering

She swallows hard, knowing that this is why he was born. It is his highest purpose for coming. Motivated by indescribable love, he has come to give himself as a burnt offering.

The little mother watches now, her heart in her throat, as a soldier stretches Yeshua's arms out on a wooden beam. Another soldier poises a six inch spike in the palm of his hand.

He lifts the heavy mallet and hammers the spike into Yeshua's tender flesh. His hand purples and numbs. A nerve severs, and his fingers draw up in a claw, as though grasping for God.

A muffled scream breaks from Miryam's lips, and Yochanan tries to shield her view. But she refuses to hide her eyes. She looks unflinchingly at the suffering of her Yeshua. She wants to share every trace of pain with the son of her heart.

After both hands are nailed, ropes are tied around his upper arms, which will keep his hands from tearing loose. Then his feet are crossed and spiked to the stipes, the vertical wooden beam.

Sadly, Miryam remembers the verse in the *Tanakh:* "They pierced my hands and feet."[113] Her thoughts slip back to the days when, as a baby, she often cupped his tiny feet in her hands and pressed

Preparing the Burnt Offering

them to her lips. Now those lovely feet are mangled and coated with gore.

She looks at his hands, recalling how she once patted her face with his palms. Now iron spikes, driven through tendons and tissue, rivet his hands to the wood.

Slowly now, with ropes and pulleys, the Lamb of God is lifted up, and the upright beam is dropped into a hole. When the wooden beam jams into the hole, excruciating pain shoots through every nerve and cell of Yeshua's body.

Miryam cringes, but as she lifts up her eyes, she sees the tender love in his eyes. Though beaten to a bloody pulp, he seems to love his enemies with his eyes. His whole being radiates love.

He looks out at the people, not with shame and condemnation, but with deep wells of love and pity. Over and over he whispers, through parched and bleeding lips, "Father, forgive them; they don't understand what they are doing."[114]

As she gazes into these eyes of wounded love, Yeshua's own words come pouring into her heart. She remembers he said, "When I am lifted up from the earth, I will draw everyone to myself."[115]

Preparing the Burnt Offering

She stands back and looks up. Though her heart is shattering within her, there is something compelling, even magnetic, about this sight.

For God has given his greatest love gift to the world, and most of all to his beloved Jewish people. It's as though, here from this blood stained hill of Golgotha, A*donai* has thundered through heaven and earth—"Behold my Lamb! He is your holocaust offering! He is forever my gift of love to you!"

Thirteen

THE CUP OF FIRE

Engulfing ADONAI's Cup

With anguished eyes Miryam looks up at her son, sagging from two beams of wood. His face is savaged, his nose bashed and bruised, one eye is nearly swollen shut. A wreath of thorns penetrates his skin and pierces into the bone of his skull.

Streams of blood seep from the punctures in his brow, clotting in his hair. Drop by drop falls from his head, running down into his eyes and ears and nose, dripping down into his beard, trickling down his throat, and mingling with the blood pouring out through gaping wounds on his chest.

She looks into his large, sad eyes and he looks into hers. Their eyes lock, and the look that passes between mother and son is too deep for words. Yeshua's heart is in his eyes. He aches for the pain

The Cup of Fire

she feels. His streaming eyes seem to plead, "Eema, please understand, even as Avraham said to his son, God has provided *himself* a Lamb."

She wants desperately to understand, but what she sees cleaves open her heart like the blade of an ax.

She looks up now at the sign above his head: "YESHUA FROM NATZERET, THE KING OF THE JEWS." It is written in Hebrew, Latin, and Greek, the primary languages of the day.

And though the cohen gadol (high priest) had insisted that Pilate change the words to "He said, I am King of the Jews," Pilate refused. "What I have written, I have written" he said stubbornly.[116] But Miryam knows there is a higher reason. ADONAI himself wants it blazed like a banner across the skies of antiquity, "This is my Son, Yeshua! He *is* the KING OF THE JEWS!"

She has always known this day would come, for ADONAI has shown her in a thousand ways that his Son would become a Lamb. Yet in her wildest imagination, she never dreamed it would be like this. Her mind spins. She reels, almost ready to faint with grief.

Yochanan reaches for her and holds her near, and then Yeshua catches their eyes. He whispers brokenly, "Mother, this is your son. . . this is your

The Cup of Fire

mother."[117] Yochanan nods, holding the little mother in his strong arms.

Suddenly thunder rumbles through the sky and the light of the sun begins to fade. For the last three hours the sun has beaten fiercely down on the little hillside outside Yerushalayim. Now the sky darkens. A strange blackness falls over the land, and an eerie silence settles over the crowd.

Yochanan tightens his grip on Miryam. She feels a frightened pulsing in her throat. Sadly she thinks, *At his birth it was midnight and the sky was bright with God's Sh'khinah. Now at his death, it is the middle of the day and the sky is black as night.*

The little mother breathes out a long painful moan as she looks up at her lonely, twisted, pierced son, hanging between heaven and earth. She can feel the edge of the sword sawing jaggedly through her soul.

She sees his face contorting with terror as a strange darkness engulfs him. He begins struggling fiercely under this heavy weight. Ropes lash his arms to the wood, preventing the spikes from tearing through his hands. But as he twists and thrashes, his hands tug against the spikes, ripping wide the wounds, releasing fresh spurts of blood.

The Cup of Fire

Yes, now ADONAI himself has laid his hands upon his Son, and, like the scapegoat of Yom Kippur, he has transferred our sins into him.[118] Then he casts him into outer darkness, bearing the weight of Isra'el's sin and the sin of all the world.

All the lust and perversion and adultery; all the pride and murder and hatred; the deception and gossip and slander and idolatry, and legalism and so much more, have been poured upon Yeshua.

Miryam winces as Yeshua flails violently under this heavy weight. He tosses like a raft on a storm-tossed sea. *Oh my son,* she silently cries, *you are tearing open the wounds on your back with every grinding spasm of your body.* But Yeshua seems oblivious to the physical pain. Something far more hideous has fallen upon him—the gruesome poison of human sin.

A picture from the *Torah* flares up in her mind. She recalls how the children of Isra'el were dying from serpent bites in the wilderness. But God told Moshe to make a brass serpent and lift it up on a pole. Then all who looked at this serpent were healed.

Could this story in the Torah, she wonders, *have also been a picture of the Son of God, carrying the snake bite of sin?*[119] *Could ADONAI have been calling his people to look upon the Lamb and be healed, even as he called the children of Isra'el to behold the one on the pole and be healed?*

The Cup of Fire

Suddenly, Yeshua's face drains chalk white. He stops writhing. His whole body stiffens. A look of horror fills his eyes. A hush falls over the crowd. Miryam's heart freezes as she sees the look on Yeshua's face. She wants to turn away but she forces herself to keep looking. *What is happening to my son now?* Every nerve and cell of her body protests as the torture seems to intensify.

He rolls his eyes upward. His eyes are inflamed, swimming with tears and swollen with grief. His eyebrows rise in shock at what he sees. He shuts his eyes tightly unable to gaze into the caverns of hell he sees opening over him.

Miryam plunges her face into her hands, overwhelmed. *What is this look of terror I see in his eyes?* Unseen by human eyes, the cup of wrath trembles in the Father's hand. This is the cup described by ADONAI in the *Tanakh* as "the cup of reeling, the bowl of my wrath."[120]

This is the cup which Yeshua pleaded with his Father to remove when blood squeezed out of the pores of his skin in the garden. This is the meaning of the second Seder cup, the Cup of Iniquity and Judgment, in the Paschal meal. This is the fulfillment of the cup of fire that Avraham held in his hand as he climbed the hill of Moriyah.

The Cup of Fire

Now Adonai tips this cup over his beloved Son. Yeshua braces himself against the horror of this oncoming flood. God's eternal punishment against sin mounts and swells and crests like a gigantic ocean wave. Then it bursts down upon the innocent Lamb.

Wave after wave after wave of Adonai's furious wrath against sin slams down upon the Son, as the *Tanach* describes, "all your surging rapids and waves are sweeping over me."[121]

What is happening to my son? she thinks. Then she gasps as she realizes — this is the cup Yeshua prayed about in the garden. This is the cup he pleaded with Adonai to remove, the cup which he finally agreed to drink. This is the cup which the *Tanakh* defined as the cup of God's holy wrath.

She watches in horror as torrents of God's wrath crash down upon the guiltless One. A rasping sigh falls from her lips as she recalls again the words of the prophet, "We regarded him as punished, stricken and afflicted by God."[122]

Over and over the judgment of Adonai against sin smashes down upon him. Yeshua is horror stricken. Terror engulfs him. The look on his face is like that of a delirious man, burning in flames of hell. Why? Because he *is* enduring hell as he drinks the dregs of the Father's cup.[123]

The Cup of Fire

For three endless hours, Yeshua drinks and drinks and drinks the contents of A‌DONAI'S cup. In this infinite moment, this hinge of all history, he has become the burning bush, which Moshe saw on Mount Horev.[124] He has become the Scapegoat, cast into outer darkness.[125] He has become the Paschal lamb, lifted on a pole and roasted over the flames.[126]

He has become David and Solomon and Eliyahu's (Elijah's) burnt offering, when fire came down from heaven.[127] He has become the fulfillment of Avraham's holocaust offering, consumed in the fire of God's wrath.

Finally it is nearing the ninth hour, or 3:00 in the afternoon, the time of the evening burnt offering. Yeshua throws back his head and looks toward heaven. Tears quiver in his eyes. Torment fills them. They drown with grief.

His mouth moves as though he wants to say something. He spoke three times in the first three hours, once to forgive, next to save a dying thief, and third to care for his mother. In these last three hours, not a word has fallen from his lips. The agony has been too deep for words. The horror of engulfing A‌DONAI'S cup has crushed his breath away.

Now he thrusts himself down on the spike in his mangled feet. The wounds rip open and blood spills down the vertical stake, pooling on the ground. He

The Cup of Fire

draws in a chestful of air and opens his mouth to speak.

Miryam and Yochanan inch in a little closer. For a moment, time stands still. The crowd hushes. Tension charges the atmosphere. Hearts thunder in every breast.

Now, with a deep, gutteral, animal-like roar, Yeshua shrieks: *"Eli! Eli! L'mah sh'vaktani?"*

The words are a mixture of Hebrew and Aramaic, his heart language, meaning, *"My God! My God! Why have you deserted me?"*[128]

The crowd stands paralyzed. Birds' songs cease midair. The wind ceases to blow. The sun still hides its face. Dark clouds, heavy with moisture, hang low as though ready to drop a load of tears.

Miryam has seen the Roman scourge plow through his flesh, thorns piercing like icepicks into his brow, spikes driving through his hands and feet, and people spitting up in his face, but "as a sheep before her shearers is silent, so he did not open his mouth."[129] Yet now, He bawls like a wounded animal. He doesn't whimper like a lamb, he roars like a lion.

Pain claws her heart as this blood-curdling howl, like a poisonous arrow, shoots up in God's face.

The Cup of Fire

"Oh ADONAI, why have you forsaken him? How could you desert him at a time when he needs you the most?" Though her mind floods with confusion, the words of David slip into her thoughts: "My God! My God! Why have you abandoned me? Why so far from helping me? So far from my anguished cries?"[130]

And with those words, the tip of the blade cuts deep into the core of Miryam's heart. She grips her chest and doubles over in pain, falling to the ground, sobbing wildly, uncontrollably.

Yochanan kneels beside her and tries to comfort her. *No! No! I must not think of myself. I must comfort him. I am his mother, his Eema. I must be strong for him,* she thinks fiercely, half crazed with grief.

Emitting a savage cry, like the screech of a wild animal protecting her young, she leaps up and stumbles to his bleeding feet. Trembling and crying, she reaches up her hands to touch him. "I'm here, Yeshua! I'm here, my Son! I won't desert you!"

She stretches up and touches her lips to his feet, smearing her face with his blood, but she doesn't care. She presses her cheek close to the wound, hoping somehow, someway he can feel her mothering touch. But she knows that by now, his feet can no longer feel. They are numb from pain and loss of blood.

The Cup of Fire

Finally, she lets go, slumping to the ground in a crumpled heap, broken and exhausted. As she lies at his feet, in a sudden flash, she sees a picture of the Akedah (the binding), when Avraham bound the hands of his son, laid him upon the altar, and lifted the dagger over him.

She sees Yitz'chak, remaining silent, for he voluntarily surrendered to his father's will. But she wonders—*surely he too must have questioned, Why, Father? Why are you slaying me? Why are you forsaking me like this?*

She sees Avraham's hand trembling violently and she can feel the agony in this father's heart. She closes her eyes, knowing—this is a picture of the Father God and his anguish for his Son. God intervened and sent a substitute ram in Yitz'chak's place, but she knows that Father God has not withheld the knife from his own Son.

He has plunged the blade of his wrath deep into the heart of his Beloved. He has set ablaze the innocent Lamb, punishing him for our sin. Yes, his "one and only" Son has been consumed as a holocaust offering, like Avraham's substitute ram.

She lifts her head and cries up to heaven, "Oh, ADONAI, my Abba, I still must ask—how could you give so deeply? How could you sacrifice your 'one

The Cup of Fire

and only' Son to pay such a monumental price for sin?"

Then through the tears, she smiles, for she knows—only one blazing purpose could compel the Father to make such a supreme sacrifice: Love—pure, undiluted, divine LOVE!

In fact, the first time the word "love" was ever used in the *Torah* was in those words from God: "Take your son, your only son, *whom you love* and sacrifice him...." Why is this so profound? Because God was showing us, through Avraham's story, the magnitude of his love.

That's why the sacrifice of his Son was the supreme expression of his love. Love has impelled him to punish his Son in our place. This is a love beyond our human understanding. It is the unfathomable, immeasurable, sacrificial love of the Father.

This is unquestionably the greatest love story of all time and eternity. It's the story of the Jewish Mashiach who stood in our place and gave himself as *Avraham's Lamb*. Above all else, it is the story of the deep, deep love of our Father God for each of us—and especially his own Jewish people.

Fourteen

THE PIERCING

Looking upon the Pierced One

On a windswept hill outside Yerushalayim, suspended between heaven and earth, the Son of God drinks the last bitter drops of A{DONAI'S} cup.

His suffering is unthinkable. His thirst insatiable. Tendons and muscles knot up in excruciating cramps. His chest rises and falls in quick, shallow gasps.

A small group of Sadducees clench their fists and gnash their teeth at him, growling like hungry wolves clawing and snapping at their prey. He is just as the *Tanakh* says, "I am a worm, not a man, scorned by everyone, despised by the people. All who see me jeer at me; they sneer and shake their heads."[131]

Yet still there are those who love him. A man in the crowd screams out, "Once I was blind, but he

The Piercing

touched my eyes and now I can see!" A widow cries, "He raised my only son from the dead!" Several wail, "Why must he die? He is our own Jewish brother!"[132]

Softly weeping at his feet, Miryam suddenly hears her son groan hoarsely. She looks back up at Yeshua. Through cracked and bleeding lips he pleads, "I thirst!"

She can only imagine the dryness of his mouth. *With no food or drink in hours and a hot fever raging through his veins, his body must be completely dehydrated,* she thinks. The *Tanakh* describes, "My mouth is as dry as a fragment of a pot, my tongue sticks to my palate."[133] Most of all, his thirst burns deep from gulping down every last drop of ADONAI'S cup of wrath.

Miryam looks around for help. "Oh, please, someone give him a drink!" she screams, but above the raucous sounds of the mob, she can barely be heard.

She sees a few calloused soldiers guzzling posca and casting dice for her son's robe. She winces as she recalls the words of the *Tanakh,* "They divide my garments among themselves; for my clothing they throw dice."[134]

A heavy wave of sadness sweeps over her, as she thinks about this robe which she had lovingly

The Piercing

made for her son out of one piece of white linen cloth. It was white and glistening and he looked stunningly handsome in it. But now it is soiled with dirt and grime and soaked with his own blood.

A young soldier hears Yeshua's plea for a drink. He grabs a reed of hyssop, stabs it into a sponge, soaks it in vinegar, and lifts it up to Yeshua.

"Why vinegar? Why not fresh water? Hasn't he suffered enough?" Miryam screams inwardly. She knows the bitter taste of vinegar will sting his cracked lips, sour his mouth, and never slake his thirst. But then she remembers the verse in the *Tanakh*, "In my thirst, they gave me vinegar to drink."[135]

But what is this? With her eyes still focused on Yeshua, she sees something unexpected. A hint of gladness seems to gleam in his eyes. Now, with his lips wet and his tongue moistened, he prepares to speak his final words.

Yeshua's eyes flash. He pushes down hard on the spike in his feet to fill his lungs with air. Then he shouts with all his might, *"It is accomplished!"*[136]

Yes, at last his work on earth has been accomplished. The monumental work of redemption is complete. The Law and the Prophets, the types and shadows of the *Tanakh* are fulfilled. The last bitter dregs of ADONAI'S cup of wrath have been emptied.

The Piercing

And because sin has been fully punished in him, now Satan has lost the battle.

Satan did not understand the *Mystery of Avraham's Lamb.* He didn't know about ADONAI'S cup. He didn't know that Yeshua would endure the flames of God's wrath, defeating the power of sin.[137] Therefore, Satan and all his demons have no more sin on which to feed.

Though behind the scenes he has been violently attacking Yeshua, now his power is broken. The "Seed of the Woman"—from the very Seed of Avraham— has crushed the serpent's head. It is just as ADONAI told Lucifer long ago in the *Torah:* "I will put animosity between you and the woman— between your descendant and her descendant; he will bruise your head, and you will bruise his heel."[138]

Now, even as ADONAI finished his work of creation on the sixth day, God finishes his work of redemption with his sixth word, *"It is accomplished!"* And now, even as ADONAI rested on the seventh day from the work of creation, Yeshua is getting ready to enter his rest with his seventh word.

He looks down searchingly, as though wanting to say something. His broken lips soundlessly form the word—"Eema." Without words, his eyes say, "Farewell, my precious mother."

The Piercing

Miryam closes her eyes and leans into Yochanan. Tears slip silently down her face as she trembles in the young talmid's arms.

Then, with one final burst, Yeshua cries, "Father, into your hands I commit my spirit!" Miryam's heart leaps when she hears him say, "Father." She lifts her eyes heavenward. *Oh ADONAI! At last his spirit is returning to you!*

As she prays, a heaving tide of love swells up within her. She can feel the Father's heart trembling with love for his one and only Son. His love pulses in her veins.

Since the night when the glory came down on the little rooftop in Natzeret, she has felt so close to the Father. They have always shared this mutual bond, a profound secret, a love for Yeshua that no one else could fully understand, not even Yosef.

Yeshua's final words still hang in the air. "Father, into your hands I commit my spirit." Then he bows his head, releases his spirit to the Father, and now it happens.

His heart breaks! It ruptures, pouring out blood and water. The *Tanakh* says, "I am poured out like water. . . . My heart has become like wax — it melts inside me."[139]

The Piercing

Suddenly thunder cracks and lightning lashes the sky. The earth roars and the ground begins to shake. It almost seems the whole universe responds to this colossal event. Lightning flashes like bright shining floodlights. Thunder claps like loud crashing cymbals. The wind whistles like shrill blaring trumpets. The ground rumbles like deep rolling drums.

It's as though ADONAI himself is announcing to Isra'el and all the world, "Behold your Jewish Mashiach! Behold the *Mystery of Avraham's Lamb* — now unveiled!

And then — as though God himself wants to emphasize this vast, massive unveiling — over in the temple, to the shock of attending cohanim (priests), the heavy veil suddenly tears in two from top to bottom.

This veil was said to be as thick as a man's hand, needing three hundred cohanim to handle it. Only the hand of God could have ripped it apart, for it symbolizes the tearing of his Son's own heart, opening the way back into the presence of God.

For a moment, Miryam turns and looks around at the frenzied mob, some rich, some poor, some dressed in elegance and some in rags.

The Piercing

The grizzled, life-scarred faces of poverty stricken people look up at Yeshua. Their eyes fill with despair, for he was their only hope. Many of them still reach out their hands to him as though hoping a miracle will drop from his lifeless hands.

But now, as the earth quakes, women scream and begin running away. Men beat their breasts in remorse. A centurion bows, takes off his helmet, and weeps. And the two who love him most stand in awe, transfixed by the compelling scene.

Just then a soldier strides up with a heavy sledge hammer, preparing to smash Yeshua's knees to make sure he cannot push down to lift his lungs for breath.

But suddenly, the skies explode with thunder and lightning. Trees on the hillside thrash and flashes of light spear the ground. The earth quakes violently, and the soldier drops the heavy mallet. It is as though HaShem himself says, "Don't you dare break a bone of my Paschal Lamb," for the *Torah* commands, "you are not to break any of its bones."[140]

Another soldier quickly draws back his spear and plunges it into Yeshua's side. The tip of the blade drives all the way up to the pericardium, the lining around his heart. Even as Moshe struck the rock and out flowed rivers of water, quenching the thirst of

The Piercing

millions, now the rock—Yeshua himself—has been struck and out flows blood and water.

Miryam stands so near that she can feel the spray of the blood and water, spurting out upon her, like a gushing fountain.[141] She can feel the warm drops of his blood showering out on her face and throat and hands. And filling her mind comes a profound passage from the *Tanakh:*

> When that day comes a spring will be opened up for the house of David and the people living in Yerushalaim to cleanse them from sin and impurity.[142]

She falls to her knees, for now she knows the spring has been opened up like a fountain in the flesh of her own son. Then she remembers the words that precede this verse in the *Tanakh*:

> I will pour out on the house of David and on the house of those living in Yerushalayim a spirit of grace and prayer; and they will look to me, whom they pierced. They will mourn for him as one mourns for an only son.[143]

This speaks of her son, the pierced Son of God, and she knows—the piercing of the heart begins when we look upon the Pierced One.

The Piercing

She presses her hand against her chest and she realizes—this wound in her heart is not a physical piercing at all. It is a love wound, a spiritual piercing, far deeper even than the pain of her own broken heart.

It's a bitter sweet piercing, like the point of a blade cutting between bone and marrow, between soul and spirit. It's a passion that burns. A holy ache.

It hurts but she knows something has been released in her. Like the tearing of the veil in the temple, a veil has been torn from her heart. It's a piercing that will unveil many other hearts.

It is just as the prophet said long ago: "A sword will pierce your own heart, too. All this will happen in order to reveal many people's inmost thoughts."[144] This piercing, she knows, has come from gazing upon the Pierced One.

Miryam breathes out a heavy sigh and looks up to heaven. Her spirit trembles as it did long ago when she first sang these words. Through the tears she whispers brokenly, "My soul magnifies ADONAI; and my spirit rejoices in God, my Savior!"

SECTION FOUR

The Seed of Avraham's Lamb Rises and Bears Fruit

And now, the seed goes into the ground and dies. This is indeed the secret recorded in the archives of eternity, established in the Torah, weaved throughout the Tanakh, infused in the second seder cup of Pesach, and hidden in the story of Avraham's Lamb.

It's the story of the Jewish Mashiach who became a holocaust Lamb. Who drank down every drop of A<small>DONAI'S</small> cup and paid the price for sin. Even more, it's the story that reveals the infinite love of God.

It's as though A<small>DONAI</small> has dipped his brush into his Son's own blood and painted his love on the canvas of his Beloved One's flesh. He has raised him up on the easel of a stake, displayed him in the gallery of Golgotha, pulled back the veil and thundered through heaven and earth—"Behold the Lamb!"

Come now and see the miracle of resurrection as the Lamb of God rises from the grave, ascends into heaven, and falls back into his Abba Father's waiting arms...

Fifteen

THE RISEN LAMB

The First Fruits from the Dead

A fresh breath of wind whispers through the cypress and cedar trees, rushing into a garden outside Yerushalayim. Olive branches bend, their delicate leaves rustling and shining. Dew drenched lilies sway in the breeze as the gust heads straight toward the garden tomb where Yeshua's body has been lain.

Reaching the boulder in front of the grave, it whiffs through the stone, then halts. It hovers over the body of Yeshua, for this is not a natural wind at all. It is a Person—the *Ruach HaKodesh* who now trembles over the body of the Son.

Lifeless and stiff, wounded and scarred, the corpse of Yeshua lays out on the slab. Even as Yonah (Jonah) spent three days in the belly of a whale, this is Yeshua's third day in the belly of the earth.[145]

The Risen Lamb

He has been buried in the wealthy Yosef of Ramatayim's tomb, for the *Tanakh* says, "in his death he was with a rich man."[146]

And now, as sunrise nears on the first day of the week, the cohanim in the temple are preparing to wave sheaves of barley before ADONAI to celebrate the Festival of First Fruits.

With deep emotion, the *Ruach HaKodesh*—the Holy Spirit—longs to be restored to the One he loves. He is especially tender and gentle and sensitive and love-filled and emotion-charged, and he loves Yeshua dearly.

Now, even as he overshadowed Miryam when she conceived, he overshadows the body of Yeshua. He has ached for this moment. Closer he draws, hovering over the body of the Son, waiting for the command of the Father.

At last, with love bursting in his heart, the Father shouts, "Now! Raise my Son as the First Fruits from the dead!"

With a mighty rush, the *Ruach HaKodesh* floods into the spirit of Yeshua, then into his soul, then through his body. The breath of God courses through his whole being, filling his lungs and quickening his heart. Glory pumps through every vein.

The Risen Lamb

Yeshua takes a deep breath. Oxygen surges through his body, pouring strength into his muscles. His eyelids flutter, then open. Slowly now he rises, lifting out of the grave clothes that enwrap him. These clothes, emptied now of their body, sink in as though by the suction of a vacuum.

Yeshua stands upright. He exhales and the whole tomb floods with the resurrection glory of the the Mashiach. The rarefied air in the tomb is thick with the presence of ADONAI. Because the veil of Yeshua's heart has been torn, the *Sh'khinah* glory, enfleshed in human skin, has been released from the container of his human body.

He is the fountain head, the reservoir, the headwaters of the *Kabod*, the heavy weighty glory of God. Like the hot molten lava of an erupting volcano, like the rock in the wilderness, struck by Moshe's rod, resurrection glory erupts and floods from the heart and soul of the Lamb.

He is indeed "the sole expression of the glory of God [the Light-being, the out-raying, the radiance of the divine]."[147]

Angels stand back in awe, stunned by his beauty. Yeshua's face shines like the morning sunrise, as the *Tanakh* says, "His brightness is like the sun, rays come forth from his hand — where his power is concealed."[148] It is just as the prophet predicted:

The Risen Lamb

"The sun of righteousness will rise with healing in its wings."[149]

Now angelic beings roll away the stone, not so that Yeshua can come out, for he could walk right through the boulder. The stone must be removed so the women and the talmidim can look in and see—the tomb is empty. Yeshua has risen as the First Fruits from the dead!

Startled, Miryam awakens and sits upright. Like the toll of a bell, her heart begins to ring. A mother usually knows when something terrible or wonderful has happened to her child. And though she can still feel the ache in her throat, raw and swollen from grieving, she knows something is in the air. She can feel it as only a mother can.

Shafts of sunshine pour in through the open window and birds trill happily in the trees outside. Life pulsates all around her. Looking around, she sees that the other women are still sleeping, exhausted from the ordeal of the last few days.

She notices, however, that something priceless is missing. It's her sacred jar of myrrh, given to her long ago by the Maji, which she has saved all these years. Then she remembers, last night amidst all the

The Risen Lamb

turmoil and trauma, Magdalene had quietly asked if she could use some of the myrrh.

Miryam looks over to the corner of the room where Magdalene sleeps. Her pallet is empty.

Rising and splashing water over her face, the little mother steps out quietly into the courtyard. The heady fragrance of spring roses, jasmine, and honeysuckle drifts through the garden.

A ram's horn in the distance announces the opening of the temple gates. She knows that people will be swarming into the temple courts, waving their first fruit sheaves of barley before A<small>DONAI</small>.

As she sits down in the morning sunlight, she ponders, *Something has happened. I know it! I can feel it!*

Suddenly she hears a shrill female voice coming up the pathway leading to the courtyard. The gate flings open and Magdalene bursts inside. Her hair is disheveled, scratches etch across her arms, but her face shines like a thousand sunbursts.

"Miryam, Miryam, he's alive! Yeshua is alive!" she shouts.

The little mother's eyes widen. Shock sweeps over her, but she can feel the glory of Yeshua emanating from Magdalene's face.

The Risen Lamb

The younger woman carries the jar of myrrh, still full and unused. Carefully setting it down, she places her hands on the mother's shoulders. With tears exploding from her eyes, she cries, "Miryam, I have seen the Lord!"

Her voice bubbles over as she proceeds to tell her story. "I hardly slept at all last night, and when finally I thought the streets would be safe, I slipped out quietly. I wanted to anoint Yeshua's body more properly with spices."

Looking down at the jar on the ground, still brimming with the sacred myrrh, she adds reverently, "I knew this myrrh was your special treasure, only to be used for Yeshuah's death."

Miryam nods, dazed by the wonder of it all.

"Thankfully, the full Paschal moon lit the way in the darkness, though I stumbled blindly to try to find the garden tomb.

"Finally, as the first streaks of grey dawn began to break over the horizon, I found it. But I was devastated! The stone had been rolled away and Yeshua's body was nowhere to be found.

"I rushed back to tell Kefa and Yochanan, shouting, 'They've taken the Lord out of the tomb, and we don't know where they have put him!'[150]

The Risen Lamb

"They came running, but they couldn't find him either. They gave up and went back in hiding with the brothers behind locked doors.

"But I just couldn't leave. My love for Yeshua held me. I was heart sick for my Mashiach."

"I understand," the little mother nods.

"Then I saw a peculiar light glowing from inside the tomb. I was terrified, but I forced myself to slip down the steps and look inside. There I saw two gleaming angels. They said, 'Why are you looking for the living among the dead?'[151]

"I caught my breath and hurried back outside, looking everywhere. I saw a gardener working in the garden and I pleaded with him to tell me where the body of my Lord had been taken.

"The gardener turned around and called my name. My heart stood still. He spoke with the warm rich tones that could only come from Yeshua."

Tears drip silently down Miryam's face as she listens.

"'Rabbani (Teacher)!' I shrieked and fell at his feet, my tears washing his wounds. And when I began to dry his feet with my hair, he put his sweet hand on my shoulder. 'Stop holding on to me,' he said, 'because I haven't yet gone to my Father. But go to my brothers and tell them I am going back to my Father and your Father, to my God and your God.'"[152]

"I dashed back into the city to the upper room where the men were hiding. I burst into the room and shouted, 'I have seen the Lord!'

"But, Miryam, they looked at me darkly, with dull eyes. I don't think they believed me. I heard one of them mutter, 'How can we believe the rantings of a woman?' I heard another say under his breath, 'And a woman of ill repute, at that!' Kefa grumbled, 'If Yeshua had truly risen, he would have come first to us, his own talmidim.'"

"I was hurt, Miryam! Simply because I am a woman, they wouldn't believe! They even brought up my past, which Yeshua has forgiven," she says, her lip quivering as angry tears spill down her cheeks.

Then brightening, she cries, her voice rising, "But I saw him! I talked to him! I know it was him!" She pauses and with pleading eyes, she asks, "Do you believe me?"

A flood of warm tears fills Miryam's eyes. "I believe you, my Child. I *do* believe you!"

Magdalene falls into Miryam's arms, sobbing like a baby. "Oh, praise be to ADONAI! I knew you would believe!"

The Risen Lamb

"I know, I know," comforts Miryam soothingly. "I haven't seen him, but I have felt his presence. From the moment I awoke this morning, I knew something wonderful had happened.

The two women weep together, wordlessly. They weep in relief. They weep from shared pain. They weep for love.

By now, awakened by the commotion, the other women gather in the courtyard, overjoyed when they hear the news. They gather around her, listening for hours to every detail of her story.

"I will never understand why he chose me to be the first to behold the risen Lord," Magdelene says humbly.

Miryam smiles. "I know why," she says. "It's because of your great hunger. Hunger kept you awake all night and drove you to the tomb alone in the dark. Hunger held you at the tomb when he seemed impossible to find. Hunger drove you to the talmidim, and even when they didn't fully believe you, your hunger drove you to us."

The women all heartily agree, hugging her and affirming her profusely. They all know how much she has been hurt, as together the sisters' hearts overflow with love and joy.

The Risen Lamb

But across town, where the brothers hide in an upper room behind locked doors, the mood is not so exuberant. A heavy gloom rests over the eleven talmidim.

One of the men says, "I don't know what to believe. Why would the Lord appear first to a woman? What do you think, Kefa (Peter)?"

Kefa lifts his tear-streaked face. He still aches with shame over his own denial of the Lord. When Yeshua needed him most, he wasn't there. Whenever he closes his eyes, he sees the eyes of Yeshua, turning and looking straight at him when he denied him for the third time in the priests' courtyard.

Even this morning, he had raced to the tomb, only to find it empty. Finally, he says hoarsely, "If he is alive, why are we too unworthy for him to come to us?"

"I do believe her!" says Yochanan firmly. All eyes turn toward the young talmid. "Magdalene wouldn't conjure up such a story unless it were true.

"But even more, when she came the first time, telling us his body was missing, I jumped up and raced toward the tomb. When I got there, I saw the boulder rolled away from the entrance. I was afraid, but I entered the tomb anyway."

The Risen Lamb

He hesitates, his eyes shining. "When I got inside the tomb, my heart was pounding so hard I thought my ribs would break, but I kept on looking around. What I saw almost took my breath away.

"There were his empty grave clothes, laying neatly folded, just like Yeshua would do." The young talmid's voice breaks, and he swallows to recover himself.

"Yeshua's body was gone, but his fragrance lingered on. I could feel his presence still filling the atmosphere. It was like a residue of his glory remained in the tomb. Like a musky perfume still permeating the air. . ."

Suddenly, his words trail off, as the heavy presence of God fills the room. Yochanan's heart jolts. Kefa looks up quickly to see what causes this stir. The disciples gasp.

Without a twist of the bolt or a creak of the locked door, the Lord himself walks into the room. Yeshua's eyes are moist. He exudes love. "Shalom aleikhem!" (Peace be unto you), he says. His smile splashes glory over everyone.

Yochanan springs to his feet. His heart hammering hard, tears washing his face. He sees Yeshua reaching out with open hands, exposing the

The Risen Lamb

gaping holes. Then He pulls back His robe and shows them the wound in his side.

The young talmid's eyes widen. His knees weaken as he looks into these deep, shining wounds. "Master!" breathes Yochanon, falling to his knees.

Yeshua lifts His nail-scarred hands and says, "Just as the Father sent me, I myself am also sending you." He breathes out upon them all, and says, "Receive the *Ruach HaKodesh!*"

Then, his eyes sparkling with love, he adds a secret for continually containing the presence of the *Ruach HaKodesh:* "If you forgive someone's sins, their sins are forgiven; if you hold them they are held."[153]

Yochanan breathes in the life of Yeshua. He drinks and drinks of the sweet presence of God. His body trembles as his whole being floods with weighty glory. He knows this is the glory which Yeshua died to give him. It's free to receive but it cost God everything. It's the resurrection glory of the Lamb.

Sixteen

THE ASCENDED LAMB

The Glorious One on the Throne

Running breathlessly through the city gate, Yochanan rushes toward the house where Miryam temporarily resides in Yerushalayim.

Forty days have passed since Yeshua's resurrection, and as he bursts into the courtyard, he thinks, *I can hardly wait to tell her what I've seen!*

Miryam stands outside, humming and busily washing clothes. When she sees him, she wipes her hands on her apron and greets him with a motherly hug. She can see by the look on the young talmid's face that he has been with Yeshua.

"Mother, I must tell you what happened this morning. Yeshua led us up the Mount of Olives.[154] We were all happily following him up the winding pathway, but I noticed an unusual air of expectancy, exuding from his whole being.

The Ascended Lamb

"Finally, he stopped and turned around toward us all. He lifted up his hands, and like a cohen gadol (high priest) coming out of the holy of holies, he prayed a b'rakhah (blessing) over us.

"Then, even as he blessed us, he slowly began to rise. I could hardly believe my eyes as the hands that bled now blessed![155]

"I watched, my heart thudding in my chest, as he rose above the olive trees, and a bright cloud came and hid him from view. Oh, Mother, it was amazing! Yeshua has ascended back to heaven, back to his Father God!"

Miryam bites her lip. "D-do you think he will ever return? Oh, Yochanan, I will miss him so much," she says trying to hold back her emotions.

"Yes, he will return! As we stood staring into the sky, we saw two men dressed in white. They said, 'You Galileans! Why are you standing, staring into space? This Yeshua, who has been taken away from you into heaven, will come back to you in just the same way as you saw him go into heaven.'"[156]

Miryam closes her eyes, letting it all soak in. She lifts her face toward heaven and envisions the scene when the Son returns to his Father.

She can almost see ADONAI, waiting in the throne room with outstretched arms. She can picture

The Ascended Lamb

Yeshua, the wounded Lamb, rushing through the outer courts of eternity, stumbling into his Father's arms. At last the wounded Son is home.

Suddenly, another scene from the story of Avraham fills her thoughts. She pictures the moment when the angel of A<small>DONAI</small> intervened, stopping him from harming his son. She had always envisioned Avraham quickly cutting the ropes that bound his son and then throwing his arms around him, weeping and praising God.

Even now, she envisions Yeshua—cut loose from the ropes of this world. She can almost picture the Father in heaven, throwing his arms around his Son and sobbing in shameless abandon.

She can hardly contain the mixed emotions she feels as she thinks of Father and Son at last together again. She imagines them weeping and laughing in boundless joy, for at last they are reunited.[157]

She knows all heaven must have surely hushed. Only the muffled laughter and cries of Father and Son can be heard: "Abba, my Abba!" "Son, my Beloved!"

And overshadowing them, the *Ruach HaKodesh* would be weeping and rejoicing with love. At Golgotha, indescribable grief had filled him as he stood back watching the Son suffer, but now he too is

The Ascended Lamb

elated over his resurrection, ascension, and reunion with the Father.

Yes now, at last, all three of them are reunited—Father, Son, and *Ruach HaKodesh*—in the throne room of Elohim. And when their tears subside, the Father wipes his eyes and lifts his mighty arm. Pointing toward his Son he thunders through eternity—"Behold the Lamb, slain from the creation of the world!"[158]

Miryam can imagine all heaven exploding in glorious worship and praise, for now he who once wore a cruel crown of thorns, wears a golden crown of glory. From robes dipped in blood to a kingly robe of splendor. From a mock scepter in his hand to a scepter of authority.

She smiles as she thinks of the incredible contrast—from the insults of men to the worship of angels. From the filth of human sin to the beauty of holiness. From abandonment by the Father to face-to-face fellowship with his Abba. From drinking ADONAI'S agonizing cup to drinking the fullness of His glorious presence.

And though she knows she will miss him terribly, she is grateful for this short time she has had with her Mashiach.

The Ascended Lamb

Yeshua has returned to the Father, but Miryam remains in Yerushalayim, for Yeshua had told them, "Now I am sending forth upon you what my Father promised, so stay here in the city until you have been equipped with power from above."[159]

Then one day, as the Festival of Shavu'ot (Pentecost) dawns in the land of Isra'el, it happens. . .

One hundred and twenty Jewish believers, including Miryam, gather together, praying in an upper room.[160] When suddenly, like the roar of a rushing mighty wind, a sound comes from heaven.

It fills the whole house and they see what looks like tongues of fire, resting on each of them. They are all filled with the *Ruach HaKodesh* and begin overflowing in tongues of worship and jubilant praise.[161]

It almost seems as though their beloved Yeshua has bent down from heaven and breathed. His fountain of glory has opened over them all. The presence of God electrifies the atmosphere. Every breath they take is filled with holiness. Life from Adonai satiates every cell of their being. It is as though heaven has come down to earth.

Miryam drinks richly of this glorious presence. She leans back against the wall, sliding to the floor and looking up to heaven. With the power of God

The Ascended Lamb

coursing over her, she recalls the night the *Ruach HaKodesh* came upon her and Yeshua was miraculously conceived.

Now she knows that the agonies of the whipping post, the terrors of Golgotha, and the piercing of her own heart were all part of Adonai's magnificent plan. Here in the glory of his presence, as the *Ruach HaKodesh* sweeps through her, all the heartaches seem to fade like smoke in the wind. Every bleeding wound in her heart fills with fathomless glory.

The years pass, during which intense persecution breaks out against the followers of Yeshua. Though the body of believers grows, all the Jewish emissaries (apostles) have been martyred, except for Yochanan. He has been banished to the Island of Patmos where an iron ball hung from a chain clamped to his ankle. Now he has been released, returning to Ephesus where the elderly Miryam lives as part of the believing community.

As soon as Yochanan finds her, he tells her what she has longed to hear. Brimming with excitement, he cries, "I saw him, Mother! I saw Yeshua!"

The Ascended Lamb

Holding her wrinkled hand, Yochanan spills out his story: "Though I was manacled in chains, I was worshipping my Lord one morning, sitting on a cliff overlooking the Aegean Sea. I could feel the ocean spray splashing my face as I watched the rising sun cast orange folds across the waters.

"Suddenly, my heart began to pound and I could feel heat upon my face, but it was not from the light of the sun. It was the *Ruach HaKodesh* who had settled down over me with a spirit of revelation. The heat increased and I could feel an intense trembling starting somewhere deep inside.

"I looked up and to my amazement, I saw heaven open before me. I could see into the throne room of God. Oh, I tell you, the sight was spectacular! Thunder peeled and bolts of lightning flashed around the throne. Rainbows of splendor flooded the eternal realm. The very atmosphere of heaven was glory. Worshippers basked in it, seraphim breathed it in, and all they could do was cry over and over, 'Holy, holy, holy!'"

Miryam's face flushes and the veins in her neck stand out, pulsating rhythmically with her heartbeat. She rocks back and forth as she eagerly drinks in every word.

"But then, a scroll was revealed which no one was worthy to open. I wept until I heard a voice cry,

The Ascended Lamb

'Look, the Lion of the tribe of Y'hudah, the Root of David, has won the right to open the scroll.' My heart leapt, and I looked, expecting to see a mighty Lion."

Yochanan's voice quivers as he says, "I squinted the eyes of my spirit and what I saw took my breath away. I saw on the throne 'a Lamb that appeared to have been slaughtered.'[162] Miryam, it was *Yeshua!*"

The little mother has been choking back her feelings, trying to contain herself, but now, in a sudden surge of emotion, a sob breaks from within. Her heart races and her whole body vibrates.

Yochanan squeezes her hand, respectfully waiting for her weeping to subside. He can only imagine how this little mother must feel as explosions of pent-up emotion erupt from her tender heart.

His voice softens. "Yes, it was Yeshua! It was our beloved Mashiach! And, Miryam, he still had deep gashes carved into his flesh, causing him to look like a wounded Lamb. But he was beautiful, Miryam! He was absolutely stunning!

"Yeshua smiled and *Sh'khinah* light drenched eternity. His eyes washed heaven with love. He lifted his arms and glory bled from every wound."

Yochanan's words explode like a fire in Miryam's heart. Her face flushes bright red and her breath comes in shallow, rapid gasps. Even as he speaks, describing the glory of the Lamb, *Sh'khinah* light floods over both of them.

"Oh, I tell you, my heart melted into a million pools when I realized that he whose eyes once spilled teardrops of sorrow, now blazed with holy fire. His hair, once soaked with clotted blood, now shone as white as fresh fallen snow. His face, once swollen and raw from patches of beard torn out, now radiated brighter than the light of the sun. His body, once stripped naked and bathed in blood, now glowed with a robe of dazzling splendor.

"I looked at his hands and feet. Now the hands that bled from nail holes, bled with infinite rays of light. It was just as the *Tanakh* says, 'His brightness is like the sun, rays come forth from his hand — that is where is power is concealed.'[163]

"The feet once spiked to a stake of timber, now gleamed like polished brass. His side, once stabbed with the blade of a spear, now released streams of glory to this earth.[164]

"Precious Mother, do you know that your son — Yeshua, the Lamb of God — is now the central sun of eternity. In fact, his splendor outblazes the sun. He stands like a fountain of brilliance. He is the lamp of all heaven, 'for the city has no need for the sun or the moon to shine on it, because God's *Sh'khinah* gives it light, and its lamp is the Lamb.'[165]

"Yes, even the seraphim had to cover their eyes with two of their wings because they stood so close to his glory. I was so overcome by this scintillating glory of the Lamb, for a moment I fell backwards on the rocks!"

Yochanan looks deep into Miryam's sweet glistening eyes, knowing how much this means to her. "Dear Mother, I must tell you that now in heaven every eye focuses on One Person—Yeshua who looks like a slain Lamb. I saw the living creatures and the twenty-four elders fall down before him and they sang a new song:

> You are worthy to take the scroll and break its seals; because you were slaughtered; at the cost of your blood you ransomed for God persons from every tribe, language, people and nation.[166]

"I looked and I saw millions upon millions of angels shouting, 'Worthy is the slaughtered Lamb to receive power, riches, wisdom, strength, honor, glory and praise!'

"And then I heard every creature in heaven and earth and under the earth and on the sea, saying,

The Ascended Lamb

'To the One sitting on the throne and to the Lamb belong praise, honor, glory and power forever and ever!' And then the four living creatures said, '*Amen!*' and the elders fell on their faces and worshipped the Lamb of God.[167]

"Oh, Miryam, at last our Jewish Mashiach—your own son—who sacrificed himself as a Lamb, is receiving the glory and honor he so richly deserves. In fact, ADONAI kept showing me throne room scenes in heaven in which Yeshua looks like a wounded Lamb. I saw the Lamb, not once or twice—*but twenty-nine* times!"[168]

She leans in closer to Yochanan, her eyes wet and shining. Clasping his hand more tightly, she says softly, "You will never know what this means to me. Thank you for bringing me this beautiful revelation—the fulfillment of *Avraham's Lamb.*

A fresh sob bursts within her as she realizes—*Now, because he was born through my own womb, there is a glorified Mashiach — the Lamb of God — on the throne! And now he has a new name, a simple Jewish name — YESHUA HaMashiach — the sweetest name on earth.*

"Oh, Yeshua, my precious and beloved Son!" Tenderly she can feel the Father's heartbeat throbbing with love in her heart. She can sense with her spirit the holy emotions of God filling her own soul.

The Ascended Lamb

With one final expression of worship, she lifts her face to heaven, and breathes the name above all names. Tears cling to her lashes as she whispers over and over again, "Yeshua... Yeshua... Yeshua...."

Epilogue

ADONAI'S LAMB

As you have read these pages, if you have felt your heart pounding hard with the truth revealed in this real life story...

If you have looked upon the Pierced One and something within you has begun to soften...

If you have gazed into his eyes and noticed the *Ruach HaKodesh* flooding over you like a warm blanket of love...

Then perhaps he is drawing you.

If you have wanted to reach up and almost touch the wounds in his hands and feet...

If your heart has been stirred by seeing Adonai's cup burning down upon him...

If you have been undone by his heart-shattering cry, *"Eli! Eli! L'mah sh'vaktani?"* . . .

Epilogue

If you have felt his *sh'khinah* glory settling softly down upon you...

Then the wonderful news is this — if you will ask him, Yeshua will come to live inside of you. Your spirit will then become his temple. The *Ruach HaKodesh* will dwell within you.

But you must be willing to humble yourself. You must earnestly admit your great need of your Mashiach. You must honestly confess to him every sin that comes to mind and ask him to wash you in his powerful, cleansing blood.

Most of all, sincerely tell him how deeply sorry you are that you did not know who he is — that he is and always has been your own Jewish Mashiach.

If tears come, let them freely flow, for they will touch the heart of ADONAI. He will not reject you. He is waiting for you with open arms.

Then say something like this, "Yeshua, I believe! I believe that you are my Jewish Mashiach. You have carried my sin; you have taken my punishment; you have poured out your blood to the death, and God has raised you from the dead.

"Right now I open wide my heart and ask you to come live inside of me. Please come in, my sweet Yeshua, and live your life in me. I am yours and you are mine forever."

Epilogue

Yes, when you call out to him, he will come. The *Ruach HaKodesh* will settle into your spirit. He will bring shalom like you've never known.

Then he will continue to open before you fathomless wells of understanding. This is probably a huge paradigm shift for you, but as you continue to behold the Pierced Son of God, great revelation will open before you.

Like the piercing of Miryam's own heart, like the ripping of the veil in the temple, your own soul will experience a glorious piercing. Let the sword of the Lamb go deep, for it will remove all scales, and cause you to see as you've never seen before.

You will behold the Lamb in all his glory, and everything within you will want to live for this one magnificent purpose: to bring Yeshua, the Lamb who was slain, the reward of his suffering for you. In all of life, there is no greater purpose.

And so concludes the greatest love story ever told. It's a story hidden from before the creation of the world. God concealed this revelation in the *Torah*, and slowly and cryptically began revealing it in the *Tanakh* (Old Testament).

This is why the *Torah* was not written on parchment, not on cowhide, not even on sheepskin. The *Torah* was written on *lambskins!* From the very

Epilogue

beginning, ADONAI was slowly unveiling to his people that their Mashiach would first come as a Lamb.

He revealed the story of his Lamb all through the *Tanakh* with the millions of slaughtered lambs. He proved it by bringing him into the world in a stable in Beit-Lechem, where lambs are born to be slain. He announced it through angels to poor shepherds in the field.

He thundered it through the land with the cry of Yochanan the Immerser. He graphically portrayed it on the hill of Golgotha. He magnificently displayed it when he raised him in splendor and seated him at his side in eternal glory.

And just to be sure you would never forget, he beautifully demonstrated the whole story in your Hebrew feasts. Yeshua was the slain Lamb at the Feast of Pesach (Passover), the buried Lamb at the Feast of Unleavened bread, the risen Lamb at the Feast of First Fruits, and then at the Feast of Shavu'ot (Pentecost), the Spirit of the Lamb—the *Ruach HaKodesh*—was poured out!"[169]

But there are three fall feasts which remain unfulfilled—Rosh-HaShanah (Shofars), Yom Kippur (Atonement), and Sukkot (Tabernacles). When these three feasts are fulfilled, it will bring a great outpouring of repentance and revival and *sh'khinah* glory upon Isra'el.

Epilogue

And this will be as "life from the dead" to the worldwide body of believers.[170] For the wall of separation—the m'chitzah—has been torn through the blood of the Lamb. And now ADONAI is making us "one new man" through the power and the glory of the Lamb.

Indeed, this story is larger than Miryam could ever have imagined. It reaches back before the creation of the world and then stretches forward into endless realms of Eternity. For Isra'el's Mashiach is the Savior of the world. He is ADONAI'S Eternal Lamb.

Now at last this timeless secret is no longer hidden. God has opened our eyes. The revelation of Isra'el's Mashiach has been revealed. It's the *Mystery of Avraham's Lamb* — at last unveiled.

ACKNOWLEDGEMENTS

Though this book has been written as a novel, it has required many years of research and teaching on the subject. Undoubtedly, the greatest resource for my study has been David H. Stern's *The Complete Jewish Bible* and his *Commentary on the Jewish New Testament*.

Though reared in a traditional Jewish home, Dr. Stern came to faith in Yeshua as his Mashiach in his late thirties. He then studied at Fuller Theological Seminary in Pasadena, California and later taught Jewish courses in the seminary.

This was meaningful to me personally because I earned my Masters and Ph.D. at Fuller as well. Now I am extraordinarily grateful for his profound Jewish scholarship, which provided much of the foundational theology in this book.

I also want to express my appreciation to Susan from England. You and your husband have been an inspiration in my life for over thirteen years. In the infant stages of this book, your finely tuned gift of hearing the *Ruach HaKodesh* caused you to urge me to focus intently on the cry of Yitz'chak (Isaac):

Acknowledgements

"Father, . . . where is the lamb?" This cry soon became the resounding question of *Avraham's Lamb*, which opened up streams of revelation and truth. I am forever grateful to you.

Special thanks to Kevin Wells for formatting the book, and also to Dr. Ruth Clay and Robin Rowan for your insightful suggestions and critique. I took all of your comments to heart and they have encouraged me enormously.

My deepest gratitude goes to my friend, LaDonna Tayler, whom God has used in healing, especially in Isra'el. When LaDonna plays her violin the *Ruach HaKodesh* often falls upon people and heals them. And now her own beautiful Jewish melodies accompany the audio version of *Avraham's Lamb*. I pray God's healing power falls on you when you listen to the audio book.

I am also forever indebted to my friends in England, many of whom are Jewish, who have read and critiqued this book. Julia and Irena, you especially challenged me to keep on digging deeper, to research the smallest details, to press on until, I hope, this work is truly pleasing to A%%DONAI%%.

Interestingly, I had tried to seek out the original artist, who painted the picture of the man holding the lamb, which is now in the clouds on the front cover of this book. While ministering in

Acknowledgements

England, I happened to ask a few friends if anyone knew who the original artist could be.

One man, a lover of Isra'el, said, "Yes, I have the original painting in my car!" He took me out to his car, and there it was. Christine Leuenberger, the artist, was his good friend, and he was on his way to Switzerland to visit her. Because of her own love for Jewish people, she was deeply honored to allow me to use this picture on the cover of *Avraham's Lamb*. And I am grateful to her for so graciously allowing it.

Thanks also to my graphic artist Kirsten Larsen for turning this into a beautiful book cover. I hope those reading the book can see the multi-level symbolic meaning of this cover.

And finally, I want to thank my dear Omaha friends and intercessors, especially Bobi, Amy, and Diane for your faithful, earnest, and strategic prayers. I know your prayers will be used by the Father to help spread this message to those who need to hear, bringing Yeshua the reward he deserves for giving his life as a Lamb.

Encounter God's Lamb

WWW.BEHOLD-MINISTRIES.ORG

Behold Ministries: Encounter God's Lamb

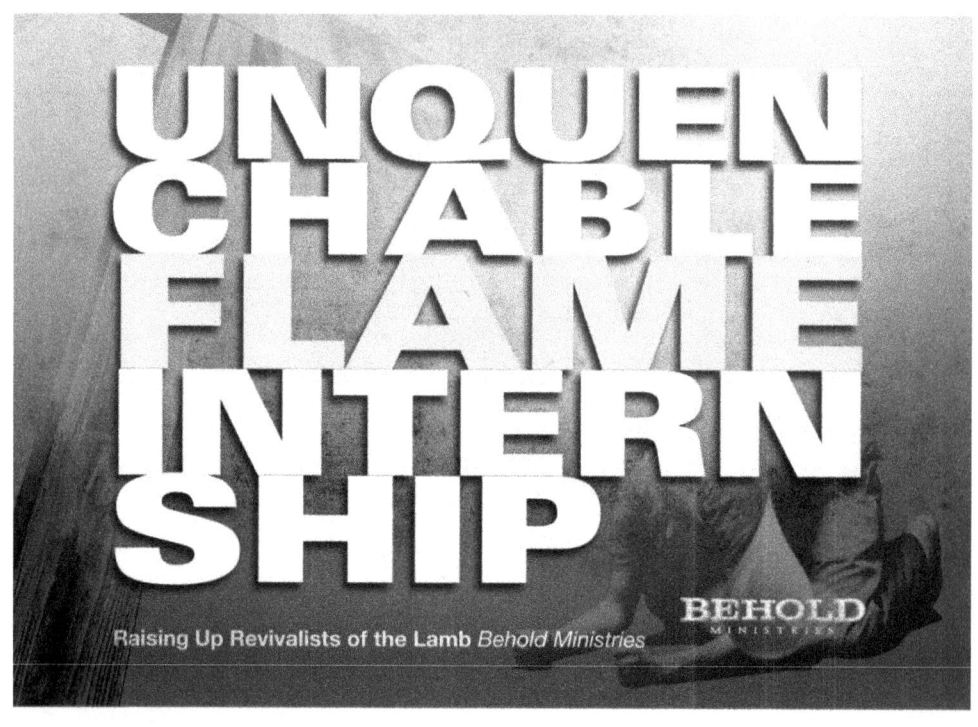

Behold Ministries: Encounter God's Lamb

Unquenchable Flame
Internships

Our purpose is to raise up revivalists who burn to bring Jesus, the Lamb of God, the reward of His sufferings. You are invited to look into the depths of the Lamb's sacrifice and the Father's cup until your heart ignites with unquenchable flames. Be grounded in solid biblical theology and move in the resurrection power of Jesus Christ. Join us on our beautiful ministry grounds on the gulf coast and experience revival.

YOU WILL:
- Be undone by Christ's sacrifice
- Find your preaching voice
- Develop fervent prayer
- Bring justice to the poor
- Mobilize for missions
- Receive impartations of revival
- Experience resurrection glory

For more information visit
www.behold-ministries.org
Or contact us via email:
beholdmininistries@outlook.com

Behold Ministries: Encounter God's Lamb

BEHOLD MINISTRIES WEEKEND SEMINARS

"Behold & Be Healed" Seminar
A weekend seminar on how to receive healing to your heart wounds by beholding the Lamb of God

"Behold & Be Ignited" Seminar
A weekend seminar on how to receive the fire of revival by beholding the Lamb of God

"Behold & Be Reconciled" Seminar
A weekend seminar which squarely faces the pain of ethnic minorities and seeks to bring healing through repentance and forgiveness

"Israel Unveiled" Seminar
A weekend seminar which uncovers our Jewish roots, unfolds the story of Avraham's Lamb, and looks at Isra'el in our current events today

OTHER BOOKS BY
DR. SANDY KIRK

UNDONE BY A REVELATION OF THE LAMB

A life-changing revelation of the glory of the Lamb

This book will give you a life-changing revelation of the Glory of the Lamb. Dr. Sandy paints a vivid picture of the Lamb of God from before the creation of the world to His crucifixion, resurrection, ascension, and glorification in eternity. This is her "Systematic Theology" Course made into warm fresh bread. Each chapter springs to life with a message that will inspire you to honor the blood of the Lamb, return to the pure gospel of Christ, and bring our Lord and Savior the reward of His suffering. You will view the awesome sacrifice of our Lord in a whole new light. Set aside everything you think you know about the crucifixion, and prepare your heart to be **Undone by a Revelation of the Lamb.**

Other Books By Dr. Sandy Kirk

THE UNQUENCHABLE FLAME

God told Moses, "The fire must be kept burning on the altar continually" (Lev. 6:13), but when the lamb ceased to be placed on the altar, the fire burned out. In the same way, when the Lamb is not central in the Church, the fire begins to smoke and eventually burn out. The Unquenchable Flame challenges the Church to bring back the central message of the Lamb until the fires of revival sweep across this land. In this day when revivals suddenly blaze and then slowly begin to smolder and die, where are the prophets like John the Baptist who will cry, "Behold the Lamb of God?" until we are "baptized in the Holy Spirit and FIRE" (John 1:29; Luke 3:16)? Where are those like the Apostle Paul who will "resolve to know nothing except Jesus Christ and him crucified" (1 Cor. 2:2) and will set the world ablaze for Christ? Where are the Apostle Peters who will brandish the sword — the Apostolic message of the Cross — until people are "cut to the heart" (Acts 2:34-35)? Where are those like John who will look into heaven until they behold the Lamb of God, then bring that vision down to earth?

THE PIERCED GENERATION

This true story shows the anguished cry pouring silently from the soul of a fatherless generation. It's a soundless scream. A cry of unparalleled pain. Read this book and look boldly into the face of pain, but then you will gaze into the face of the One who took your pain. You'll discover God's answer to the heartache of a whole generation. The Holy Spirit will carve a love wound into your heart, filling it with the fire of revival and igniting you as a revivalist of the Lamb. He will wipe away every scar, leaving only one. He will pierce your heart forever with a revelation of the Lamb. That's why we call this book THE PIERCED GENERATION.

Other Books By Dr. Sandy Kirk

THE GLORY OF THE LAMB

Come look through John's eyes as he meditates on the Lamb of Glory before creation, all through the Old Testament, in the days of His flesh on earth, when He was lifted up at His crucifixion, when He drank the Father's Cup of eternal wrath, and ascended back into God's arms. From glory to glory, from before creation to His exaltation, from Eternity past to Eternity future — this is the story of the glory of Christ — God's eternal Lamb. Many testify they were so undone by this book, it caused a continual "piercing" in their hearts. When they saw for the first time the depths of the Cup Jesus drank, a passion for the Lamb ignited and the fire has never dimmed. It is the cornerstone book of this entire ministry (McDougal, 2004).

Other Books By Dr. Sandy Kirk

BETHLEHEM'S LAMB

Bethlehem's Lamb tells the story of a young Jewish girl, clinging to her God in the midst of heart-rending pain, persecution, and wounded love. It explores the raw human emotions of each of the characters in the Nativity, rekindling the beauty and glory of Christmas. In this greatest love story of all time, you will read of the love of a man and a woman. The love of parents for their daughter. The love of a mother for her baby. The love of a Father for His only Son. The love of God's Son for you and me. It is the most exquisite love story of all human history, and through this story you will be inspired to give more freely, to love more deeply, and to worship more sincerely.

Bethlehem's Lamb is also available as an audio book.

Other Books By Dr. Sandy Kirk

ADDITIONAL BOOKS BY DR. SANDY KIRK

Rivers of Glory

The Masterpiece

A Revelation of the Lamb for America

America Ablaze

India Ablaze

The Pain (booklet)

The Pain in an African Heart (booklet)

The Mystery of Avraham's Lamb (Audio book)

The Wounded Soldier, and Wounded Soldier (Audio book)

"Revivalists of the Cross" (Glory of the Lamb) DVD SERIES

Children's Books:

Would Jesus Eat His Vegetables?

How Would Jesus Act at Bedtime?

Would Jesus be a Bad Sport?

To order, visit us online:

www.behold-ministries.org/bookstore

ENDNOTES

SECTION ONE: *PREPARING THE SEED OF AVRAHAM'S LAMB*

Chapter One: Avraham's Lamb

[1] Genesis (*B'resheet*) 22:2, *Complete Jewish Bible (CJB)*. This exact spot would someday be the location of the magnificent temple of Solomon in Yerushalayim (Jerusalem). And though this would take place hundreds of years later, God was revealing the infinite significance of this place on Mount Moriyah.

[2] See Leviticus (*Vayikra*) 1:1-17 to read the details of the burnt offering.

[3] Genesis (*B'resheet*) 22:7-8, *CJB*

[4] The *Tanakh* says that the temple in Jerusalem would be built here (2 Chronicles 3:1, [*Divrei-HaYammim Bet*]).

[5] This binding is called the *Akedah*, referring to the binding of Yitz'chak (Isaac) by his father.

[6] This story of the binding of Yitz'chak (Isaac) is read in the synagogue as part of the liturgy for the second day of *Rosh-Hashanah* (David H. Stern, *Jewish New Testament Commentary*, p. 711).

[7] Genesis (*B'resheet*) 22:11-12, *CJB*

[8] Genesis (*B'resheet*) 22:13, *Tree of Life Version of the Holy Scriptures (TLV)*. Wild myrtle bushes and juniper trees are indigenous to this area, so it is hypothesized that these could be the "thicket" to which Moshe (author of Genesis) referred.

[9] Genesis (*B'resheet*) 22:16-18, *CJB*

[10] Genesis (*B'resheet*) 22:14, *TLV*

Endnotes

[11] Today, the rock on which Yitz'chak was almost slain has been covered by the Dome of the Rock, a Muslim mosque in Jerusalem.

[12] See 1 Chronicles (*Divrei-HaYammim Alef*) 21:24-25; see 2 Chronicles (*Divrei-HaYammim Bet*) 3:1.

SECTION TWO: *THE SEED OF AVRAHAM'S LAMB IS BORN*

[13] In the *Torah* the descendants of Avraham were first called Hebrews. After his grandson Ya'akov (Jacob) was given by God the name "Isra'el," they also became known as the Children of Isra'el. The Hebrews and the Isra'elites became known as "Jews" (from Judah) after the kingdom divided and the southern kingdom of Y'hudah (Judah) settled in the land. Today "Jew" refers to anyone who is a descendent of Avraham through the line of Yitz'chak and Ya'akov (Jacob). Traditionally Jewish standing passes through the mother, not the father.

Chapter Two: Gavri'el's Promise

[14] Genesis (*B'resheet*) 22:16-18, *CJB*

[15] Luke 1:28, *TLV*

[16] Luke 1:12-20.

[17] Luke 1:31, *TLV*

[18] Luke 1:32-33, *CJB*

[19] 2 Samuel *(Sh'mu'el Bet)* 7:12-13, *CJB*

[20] Luke 1:34

[21] Luke 1:35, *CJB*

[23] Luke 1:38, *CJB*

[24] Betrothal can only be broken through filing papers of divorce, and if adultery is the cause, the Law required that the person who sinned must be stoned to death. However, this action was rarely taken in later years. Moshe (Moses) wrote, "This way you

will expel such wickedness among you."Deuteronomy *(D'varim)* 22:21-22, *CJB*. See David H. Stern, *Jewish New Testament Commentary* (Clarksville, M D: Jewish New Testament Publications, 1992), p. 3.

Chapter Three: Midnight *Sh'khinah*

[25] Yeshua may have been conceived around Hanukkah or Feast of Tabernacles or Passover. It is not wise to be dogmatic about the date, but in this story, he will be conceived around Hanukkah and born around Tabernacles.

[26] Luke 1:35, *CJB*

[27] Luke 1:31

Chapter Four: Miryam's Tehillah

[28] It was from eighty to one hundred miles to the hill country in Judea, which took three to four days by foot or caravan (Hughes, *LUKE*, Vol 1, p. 40).

[29] Luke 1:43, *CJB*

[30] Luke 1:44, *CJB*

[31] Luke 1:45, *CJB*

[32] Luke 1:46-55, *CJB*

[33] Luke 1:13, *CJB*

[34] Luke 1:20, *CJB*. Myriam had also asked the angel "How can this be since I am a virgin?" But hers was a question of physiology because she had not slept with a man. Z'kharyah actually questioned the veracity of the angel—the truth of his message.

[35] Matthew (Mattityahu) 1:17

[36] Malachi (*Mal'akhi*) 3:1,*CJB*

[37] Isaiah *(Yesha 'yahu)*40:3, *TLV*

[38] Isaiah *(Yesha 'yahu)* 9:6-7, *TLV*

Chapter Five: Yosef's Dream

[39] Deuteronomy *(D'varim)* 22:23-24, *CJB*

[40] Matthew *(Mattityahu)* 1:20, *CJB*

[41] Matthew *(Mattityahu)* 1:21, *CJB*

[42] Yeshua means Jehovah saves. Jesus is the Greek rendering of the Hebrew name for Joshua.

[43] David Stern explains that there have been at least fifty messianic pretenders in the last 2,000 years of Jewish history. None of them met the criteria laid out in the *Tanakh* about messianic identity except Yeshua, and he met all the criteria recorded in the *Tanakh*.

[44] Micah *(Mikhah)* 5:1, *CJB*

[45] Isaiah *(Yesha'yahu)* 7:14, *TLV*

Chapter Six: The Baby's Cry

[46] The name "Jew" comes from Y'udah (Judah). This was the tribe which had been released from captivity in Babylon, most of which had returned to Isra'el. Since the scattering of the ten northern tribes, the majority of people in the land are from the tribe of Y'udah. They too will be journeying to the City of David, the place of their lineage.

[47] "It's the wonder of the ages, as Michael Brown says, "This is a profound and wonderful mystery, but one that meets us right where we are: the infinite and eternal God, who sits enthroned in heaven, who fills the universe, who moves throughout the earth by His Spirit, also visited us in a person of his Son, born into this world and given the name Yeshua. And when we see him, we see God" (Michael Brown, *The REAL Kosher Jesus,* p. 137).

Chapter Seven: Beit- Lechem's Lamb

[48] Luke 2:11, *TLV*

[49] Luke 2:12, *TLV*

[50] Luke 2:13-14, *TLV*

[51] Luke 2:12, *TLV*

Chapter Eight: Bloodbath in Beit- Lechem

[52] Jewish philosopher Martin Buber said, "We must overcome the superstitious fear which we harbor about the Messianic movement of Jesus, and we must place the movement where it belongs, namely, in the spiritual history of Judaism" (Martin Buber, "Three Talks on Judaism," translated by Paul Levertoff in "Jewish Opinions About Jesus" *Der Weg* 7, no. 1 [January-February, 1933], p. 8; cited in Michael Brown, *The REAL Kosher Jesus*, p. 23.

[53] Leviticus (*Vayikra*) 12:8, *CJB*

[54] Torah says: "a one-year old lamb for a burnt offering and a young pigeon or turtledove for a sin offering. . . . But if she cannot afford a lamb, then she shall take a pair of doves or two young pigeons. . . . and the *cohen* shall make atonement for her, and she shall be clean" (Leviticus [*Vayikra*] 12:6, 8, *CJB*).

[55] "The more wealthy brought a lamb for a burnt offering, the poor might substitute a turtle-dove, or a young pigeon. . . . The substitution of the latter for a young lamb was expressly designated 'the poor's offering'" (Alfred Edersheim, *Life and Times*, pp. 195, 196).

[56] Edersheim writes, "And now the priest once more approached her, and sprinkling her with the sacrificial blood, declared her cleansed. Her 'firstborn' was next redeemed at the hand of the priest with five shekels of silver" (Alfred Edersheim, *The Temple* [Grand Rapids, MI: Kregel Publications, 1973], p. 222).

[57] Luke 2:34, *CJB*. This song of Shim'on (Simeon) is known as the Nunc Dimmitis.

[58] Isaiah *(Yesha 'Yahu)* 42:6, *CJB*

[59] Luke 2:35, *CJB*

[60] Numbers *(B'Midbar)* 24:17, *CJB*

[61] According to David Stern, the Maji were not simply magicians or astrologers. "They were sages, wise men, often in positions of responsibility but sometimes commanding respect because of their wisdom even when not holding office. These Magi came from the Medo-Persian Empire or Babylon" (David H. Stern, *Jewish New Testament Commentary,* p. 9).

[62] See Matthew (Mattityahu) 2:3-6, *CJB*

[63] SeeMatthew (Mattityahu) 2:9-10, *CJB*

[64] Matthew (Mattityahu) 2:9-10, *CJB*

[65] Hosea *(Hoshea)* 11:1, *CJB*

[66] Jeremiah *(Yirmeyahu)* 31:14, *CJB*

[67] Luke 2:35, *CJB*

Chapter Nine: "Where Is the Lamb?"

[68] The three major feasts in Isra'el, to which all the Jewish men were required to celebrate "before the Lord" at the temple in Jerusalem were Passover, Pentecost (Feast of Weeks), and Tabernacles. Apparently Yosef had attended the latter two on his own, but Miryam had always attended Passover with him (see Luke 2:41).

[69] Genesis *(B'resheet)* 22:2, *CJB*. This exact spot would someday be the location of the magnificent temple of Solomon in Yerushalayim (Jerusalem). And though this would take place hundreds of years later, God was revealing the infinite significance of this place on Mount Moriyah.

[70] See Leviticus *(Vayikra)* 1:1-17 to read the details of the burnt offering.

[71] Jewish historian Alfred Edersheim writes, "The priests drew a threefold blast from their silver trumpets. Altogether the scene was most impressive. All along the Court up to the altar of burnt-offering priests stood in two rows, the one holding golden, the other holding silver bowls. In these the blood of the Paschal lambs, which each Isra'elite slew for himself (as representatives of the company at the Paschal Supper), was caught up by a priest, who handed it to his colleague, receiving back an empty bowl, and so the bowls with the blood were passed up to the priest at the altar, who jerked it in one jet at the base of the altar" (Edersheim, *The Temple: It's Ministry and Services as they were at the Time of Jesus Christ* [Grand Rapids, MI: Kregel Publications, 1997], p. 149).

[72] Edersheim writes, "Meanwhile the crowd came down from the Temple Mount, each bearing on his shoulders the sacrificial lamb, to make ready for the Paschal Supper. . . . The Paschal lamb was roasted on a spit made of pomegranate wood, the spit passing through from mouth to vent" (Edersheim, *The Temple,* pp. 152, 154).

[73] Exodus (Sh'mot) 12: 6-10, *CJB*

[74] Jewish people call the lamb at Passover the Paschal lamb.

[75] See Mattityahu (Matthew) 2:16, *CJB*

[76] Luke 2:48, *CJB*

[77] Luke 2:49, *CJB*

SECTION THREE: *THE SEED OF AVRAHAM'S LAMB DIES*

Chapter Ten: Behold the Lamb

[78] See John (*Yochanan*) 1:32, *CJB*

[79] Luke 3:22, *CJB*

[80] John (*Yochanan*) 1:29, KJV, also John (*Yochanan*) 1:32. Charles Spurgeon said that this one sermon by John the Baptist (Yochanan the Immerser) is the single greatest sermon ever

preached. He wrote, "To meditate much on the Lamb of God is to occupy your mind with the grandest subject of thought in the universe" (Charles H. Spurgeon, "Behold the Lamb," Spurgeon's Expository Encyclopedia, Vol. 3 [Grand Rapids, MI: Baker Book House, 1977], p. 110).

[81] Genesis (*B'rsheet*) 22:13, *CJB*

[82] Exodus (*Sh'mot*) 12:10, *CJB*

[83] David Stern writes, "The central event of the original Passover was the slaughter by each Jewish family of a lamb 'without blemish or spot,' whereupon God spared the firstborn sons of the Isra'elites but slew those of the Egyptians. When Yochanan the Immerser speaks of Yeshua as the 'lamb of God' (Yn 1:29), he is invoking both Temple and Pesach imagery" (David H. Stern, *Jewish New Testament Commentary*, p. 77.

[84] Isaiah *(Yesha 'Yahu)* 53:7, *CJB*

[85] Matthew (*Mattityahu*) 5:17, *CJB*

[86] John (*Yochanan*) 1:14, *CJB*. You and I could step outside and look up at the sun in the sky until our eyes burn blind. But we could lift our eyes to the shining face of the Lamb of God, and our eyesight will purify, our gaze grows stronger, our vision clears, and our heart burns bright with his glory. He is indeed the light of life, for there is life in a look at the Lamb.

[87] Luke 9:31, *CJB*

Chapter Eleven: ADONAI'S Cup

[88] Luke 22:15, *CJB*

[89] David Stern said, "The third of the four cups... corresponding to Exodus 6:6, 'I will redeem you.' Thus Yeshua used the 'cup of redemption,' as the third cup is called to inaugurate the new covenant which redeems from the 'Egypt' of bondage of sin to all who trust in God and his Messiah" (Stern, *Commentary on the Jewish New Testament*, p. 144.

Endnotes

[90] Matthew *(Mattityahu)* 26:20-29, *CJB*. David Stern writes, "The final and fullest meaning for *Pesach* will be revealed after the return of Yeshua the Messiah to rule in glory."

[91] Matthew *(Mattityahu)* 26:39, *CJB*

[92] The Greek of "drops of blood" is *thrombos,* meaning "thick clots of blood" (Luke 22:44).

[93] Jeremiah *(Yirmeyahu)* 25:15, *CJB*

[94] Psalms *(Tehillim)* 75:8, *CJB*

[95] Isaiah *(Yeshu'yahu)* 51:17. *CJB*

[96] Isaiah (*Yesha 'Yahu*) 51:22. *TLV*

[97] Isaiah (*Yesha 'Yahu*) 53:4-5, *CJB*

[98] Psalms *(Tehillim)* 41:9, *CJB*

[99] Matthew *(Mattityahu)* 26:52-53, *CJB*

[100] John (*Yochanan*) 18:11, *CJB, Commentary on the Jewish New Testament,* p. 206

[101] Zechariah *(Z'kharyah)* 12:7, *CJB*

[102] Isaiah (*Yesha 'Yahu*) 50:6b, *CJB*

Chapter Twelve: The Burnt Offering

[103] Isaiah (*Yesha 'Yahu*) 50:6a, *CJB*

[104] Micah (*Mikhah*) 4:14, *CJB*

[105] See Matthew 27:27-31; it is believed that the sign actually read, "King of Y'huda."

[106] Isaiah 52:14, *TLV*

[107] For the burnt offering, the Torah requires, "If his offering is from the flock, . . . he must offer a male without defect" (Vayikra [Leviticus] 1:10, *CJB*).

[108] Vayikra (Leviticus) 1:12, *CJB*

Endnotes

[109] Unknown to her, in that moment of raw horror, Yeshua will be identifying with the future suffering of his own Jewish people.

[110] Isaiah (*Yesha 'Yahu*) 53:3, *CJB*

[111] In the scholarly *Commentary of the Old* Testament, C. F. Keil writes, "Mount Moriah, upon which under the legal economy all the typical sacrifices were offered to Jehovah; upon which also, in the fullness of time, God the Father gave up His only-begotten Son as an atoning sacrifice for the sins of the whole world, that by this one true sacrifice the shadows of the typical sacrifices might be rendered both real and true" (C. F. Keil and F. Delitzsch, *Commentary of the Old Testament, The Pentateuch,* Vol. 1 [Peabody, MA: Hendrickson Publishers, 2011],Pp. 161-162.

Concerning the location of Golgotha, or Calvary as it is called in Latin, Matthew Henry writes, "It is observable that the temple, the place of sacrifice, was afterwards built upon this mount Moriah (2 Chronicles 3:1); and mount Calvary, where Christ was crucified, was not far off" (Matthew Henry, *Matthew Henry's Commentary on the Whole Bible,* Vol. 1: Genesis to Deuteronomy [McLean, VA: MacDonald Publishing Company, 1706], p. 140).

[112] Every morning a pure lamb was sliced in pieces for the burnt offering. At 9:00 am, the third hour, the pieces of lamb's meat were cast down and consumed in fire on the altar. And every evening, at 3:00 pm, the ninth hour, another lamb was sliced in pieces and consumed on the altar (see Leviticus [*Vayikra*] 1:10-13.

[113] The Septuagint renders Psalm 22:16 as "They pierced my hands and feet."

[114] Luke 23:34. The Greek indicates he said this continuously. But notice he didn't say, "I forgive them," because he had already forgiven them. He was asking God the Father to forgive

Endnotes

them, rather than taking revenge on them. I believe this shows, once more, his great love for his own Jewish people as well as all who will receive him as Savior, for we all nailed Yeshua to the cross.

[115] John (*Yochanan*) 12:32, *CJB*

Chapter Thirteen: The Cup of Fire

[116] John (Yochanan) 19:19-20, *CJB*

[117] John (Yochanan) 19:26-27, *CJB*

[118] In the *Torah* God told Moshe: "Aharon (Aaron) is to lay both his hands on the head of the live goat and confess over it all the transgressions, crimes and sins of the people of Isra'el; he is to put them on the head of the goat and then send it away into the desert with a man appointed for the purpose. The goat will bear all their transgressions away to some isolated place, and he is to let the goat go in the desert" (Leviticus [Vayikra] 16:21-22, *CJB*.

[119] Numbers (B'Midvar) 21, *CJB*

[120] Isaiah (*Yeshu 'yahu*) 51:22, *TLV*

[121] Psalms (*Tehillim*) 42:7, *CJB*

[122] Isaiah (Yesha 'yahu) 53:4-5, *CJB*

[123] This is why Yeshua warned so much about hell when he preached. He knew the price he would pay when he endures the wrath of God in our place. He wanted us to understand the magnitude of his sufferings for us. He knew he would plummet the abysmal depths of human pain, but he would descend far deeper by draining every drop of God's eternal wrath and punishment.

[124] Exodus *(Sh'mot)* 3:1-3, *CJB*

[125] Leviticus (*Vayikra*) 16:21-22, *CJB*

[126] Have you ever wondered why God told Moshe that every bit of the lamb for Passover must be roasted? "They are to eat the meat that night, roasted over a fire. . . . Do not eat any of it raw or boiled with water, but only roasted with fire. . . . Whatever remains until morning you are to burn with fire" (Exodus [Sh'mot] 12:8-10]). Why couldn't the Passover lamb be baked or boiled or cooked? Why only roasted over the fire? Because *ADONAI'S* own Son would be roasted over the fires of God's wrath on Golgotha. He would be burned in the flames of eternal punishment when he drinks the Father's cup.

[127] The fire came down on the burnt offering at Moshe's tabernacle in Leviticus (Vayikra) 9:24, at David and Solomon's burnt offering on the temple mount in 2 Chronicles (Divrei-HaYamim Bet) 7:1, and on Mount Carmel with Elijah in 1 Kings (M'lakhim Alef) 18:36-38 as well as other places in the *Tanakh*. This was a foreshadowing of the fire of God's wrath—Adonai's cup—pouring down on Yeshua.

[128] Matthew *(Mattityahu)* 27:46, *CJB*

[129] Isaiah (Yesha 'yahu) 53:7, *CJB*

[130] Psalms *(Tehillim)* 22:1, *CJB*

Chapter Fourteen: The Piercing

[131] Psalm *(Tehillim)* 22: 7- 8 (6-7), *CJB*

[132] "Someone will ask him, 'What are these wounds between your hands?'—and he will answer, 'those that I received in the house of my friends'" (Zechariah [Z'kharyah] 13:6, TLV.

[133] Psalm *(Tehillim)* 22: 16 (15), *CJB*

[134] Psalm *(Tehillim)* 22: 19 (18), *CJB*

[135] Psalm *(Tehillim)* 69:22 (21), *CJB*

[136] John (Yochanan) 19:30, *CJB*

[137] It's not that we are not able to sin, but now we are able not to sin.

[138] Genesis (*B'resheet*)3:15, *CJB*

[139] Psalms (*Tehillim*) 22:15 (14), *CJB*

[140] Exodus (*Sh'mot*) 12:46, *CJB*

[141] Dr. Truman Davis states, "There was an escape of watery fluid from the sac surrounding the heart and the blood of the interior of the heart. This is another conclusive postmortem evidence that Jesus died, not the usual death of crucifixion death by suffocation, but of heart failure due to shock and constriction of the heart by fluid in the pericardium" (C. Truman Davis, "A Physician's Look at the Crucifixion" *Arizona Medicine*, Vol. 22, No. 3, March 1965). Leon Morris adds, "William Stroud wrote that it meant a physically ruptured heart, with the result that 'the blood separates into its constituent parts so as to present the appearance commonly termed blood and water'" (Leon Morris, *Reflections on the Gospel of John* [Peabody, MA: Hendrickson Publishers, Inc., 2000], pp. 674-675.

[142] Zechariah (*Z'kharyah*) 13:1, *CJB*

[143] Zechariah (*Z'kharyah*) 12:10, *CJB*

[144] Luke 2:35, *CJB*

SECTION FOUR: *THE SEED OF AVRAHAM'S LAMB RISES AND BEARS FRUIT*

Chapter Fifteen: The Risen Lamb

[145] See the book of Jonah (Yonah). Yeshua's body went into the tomb on Friday, before sunset on Shabbat (Sabbath), which was the first day; from sunset to sunset on Shabbat was the second day; and from sunset to the time of his resurrection before dawn was the third day.

[146] Isaiah (*Yesha 'Yahu*) 53:9, *CJB*

[147] Hebrews 1:3, *Amplified Bible*

[148] Habakkuk (*Havakuk*) 3:4, *CJB*

Endnotes

---

[149] Malachi (*Mal'akhi*) 3:20 (4:2), *CJB*

[150] John (*Yochanan*) 20:2, *CJB*

[151] Luke 24:5, *CJB*

[152] John (*Yochanan*) 20:17, *CJB*

[153] John (*Yochanan*) 20:21-23, *CJB*

Chapter Sixteen: The Ascended Lamb

[154] This is the mount where Yeshua made his triumphal entry into Yerushalayim; now he is about to make his triumphal entry into heaven. Even as the *Sh'khinah* lifted off the temple and rose up to heaven from this same mount, he who embodies the glory of God is about to ascend from the Mount of Olives.

See Ezekiel (*Yechezkiel*) 11 for a description of the glory lifting off the temple and ascending out over the mountain east of the city, which is the Mount of Olives. It is also from this same mount that Yeshua will touch down when he returns in his second coming (see Zechariah [Z'kharyah] 14:4).

[155] Luke 24:50-51, *CJB*

[156] Acts 1:11, *CJB*

[157] As Father and Son embraced, all the sadness of separation, the agony of their suffering, the anguish of drinking the cup, the ecstasy of the resurrection, and the bliss of reunion must have all converged in one gigantic wave of holy emotion.

[158] This is taken from Revelation 13:8, *CJB*

[159] Luke 24:50-51, *CJB*

[160] Luke 24:49, *CJB*. For forty days Yeshua has walked on earth with his talmidim, but he has urged them all not to leave Yerushalayim until they have received the promise of the Father: He said, "For Yochanan used to immerse people in water; but in a few days you will be immersed in the *Ruach HaKodesh!*" (Acts 1:5). Although he had given them a foretaste,

when he breathed on them in the upper room, now he says, "But you will receive power when the *Ruach HaKodesh* comes upon you; you will be my witnesses both in Yerushalayim and in all Y'hudah and Shomron (Samaria), indeed to the ends of the earth" (Acts 1:8).

[161] Acts 2:1-4, *CJB*

[162] Revelation 5:5-6, *CJB*

[163] Habakkuk 4:3, *CJB*

[164] In the B'rit Hadashah (New Testament), see Revelation 1:13-16, *CJB*

[165] Revelation 21:23, *CJB*

[166] Revelation 5:9, *CJB*

[167] Revelation 5:11-14, *CJB*

[168] John saw Him as a wounded Lamb in heaven twenty-nine times: Rev. 5:6; 5:8; 5:12; 5:13; 6:1; 6:7; 6:16; 7:9; 7:10 ;7:14; 7:17; 12:11; 13:8; 14:1; 14:4; 14:4; 14:10; 15:3; 17:14; 17:14; 19:7; 19:9; 21:9; 21:14; 21:22; 21:23; 21:27; 22:1; and 22:3. It is also important to note again that John saw Jesus described as a "Lion" one time (Rev 5:5); as the "Word of God" one time (Rev 19:13); as a "King" three times (Rev 15:3; 17:14; 19:16); and as the "Morning Star" one time (Rev 22:16), but He is described as a "Lamb" twenty-nine times.

Epilogue: A*DONAI* 's Lamb

[169] Yeshua was crucified on the Jewish Festival of Pesach, as the Passover Lamb. He was buried on the feast of Unleavened Bread as sin was buried in him. He rose from the dead on the Jewish Festival of First Fruits as the First Fruits from the dead. And now he has poured down the *Ruach HaKodesh* on the Jewish Festival of Shavu'ot (Pentecost), as he writes his law of love on the tablet of human hearts.

[170] Romans 11:15, *CJB*

www.ingramcontent.com/pod-product-compliance
Lightning Source LLC
Chambersburg PA
CBHW071311110426
42743CB00042B/1275